P9-DHN-401

TOPIC GUIDE

INTRODUCTION

Brigham Young, the "Lion of the Lord," magnified his name and his calling as a special witness for the Lord Jesus Christ throughout his long and challenging life. From the moment of his conversion he threw himself heart and soul into the work of the kingdom; never doubting, faltering, or looking back upon the world with regret or longing, but always reaching upward, drawing excitement and purpose from the things of the Spirit, while at the same time loving, encouraging, and serving his fellow Saints.

Elder Neal A. Maxwell observed that "Brigham Young hungered for the word in his early discipleship. While he was not easily impressed by anyone, his regard for Joseph was deep, and it never left him. Of this prophet-pupil relationship, Brigham, now himself the prophet, said: 'An angel never watched Joseph closer than I did, and that is what has given me the knowledge I have today. I treasure it up, and ask the Father in the name of Jesus,

to help my memory when information is wanted'"
(Neal A. Maxwell, *Lord Increase Our Faith* [Salt
Lake City: Bookcraft, Inc., 1994], p. 106).

With such a rich source to draw upon,
mingled with his own distinct vision and
unfailing faith, Brigham set about teaching,
instructing, admonishing, and inspiring the
Saints. The hundreds of his sermons that were
recorded and preserved leave us with no doubt
that "Brother Brigham" had something to say
about everything. He was oftentimes straightfor-
ward, to the point, and pragmatic; but he could
also be eloquent, and even poetic, despite his lack
of formal education, or his surprising lack of
confidence in himself when speaking in public.
Surely the same zeal and fervent depth of his own
convictions that sang then through the words he
uttered make them leap to life today as we read
and realize their power and relevancy in our
different and multi-challenging day.

In the scriptures we read, "Of the abundance of
the heart [the] mouth speaketh" (Luke 6:45).
Brigham's heart abounded with love for the God

8

he served, for the Prophet of the Restoration, for his family, and for the Saints. In modern-day revelation to Joseph Smith, the Lord tells his Saints that he "requireth the heart and a willing mind" (D&C 64:34). He found both in his servant, Brigham Young.

Brigham's words can, in turn, inspire and motivate us. By heeding his counsel, we, too, may find ourselves desiring to purify our lives so that we may be of use in the kingdom; so that we might magnify the precious truths given to us; so that we might experience the joy and eventual salvation that is our birthright as sons and daughters of an all-wise, all-knowing, all-loving God.

Susan Evans McCloud

Provo, Utah—April 1998

Brigham Young

Prophet, Seer, and Revelator

1 June 1801	Born inWhittingham, Widdham County, Vermont
15 April 1832	Baptized a member of the Church of Jesus Christ of Latter-day Saints
14 February 1835	Ordained a member of the Quorum of Twelve Apostles
6 April 1840	Arrives in Liverpool to preside over British Mission
1 July 1841	Arrives in Nauvoo at completion of mission

27 December 1847	Sustained as President of the Church at Kanesville, Iowa
1851	Becomes governor of Utah Territory
29 August 1877	Dies in Salt Lake City, Utah at age of 76
2 September 1877	A Sabbath: Brigham's funeral, and burial in private family plot

BIBLIOGRAPHY OF SOURCES USED

Andrus, Hyrum L. & Helen Mae, *They Knew the Prophet.* Salt Lake City: Bookcraft, 1974.

Arrington, Leonard J., *Brigham Young: American Moses.* Urbana and Chicago: University of Illinois Press, 1986.

Deseret News (Weekly) [DNW]. Salt Lake City: 1854, 1860.

Gates, Susa Young and Widtsoe, Leah D., *The Life Story of Brigham Young.* New York: The MacMillan Co., 1931.

Jessee, Dean C., ed., *Letters of Brigham Young to His Sons.* Salt Lake City: Deseret Book, 1974.

Journal of Discourses (JD), 26 vols. London: Latter-day Saints' Book Press, 1980.

McCloud, Susan Evans, *Brigham Young: An Inspiring Personal Biography.* American Fork: Covenant Communications, 1996.

Spencer, Clarissa Young, *Brigham Young at Home.* Salt Lake City: Deseret Book, 1963.

Widtsoe, John A., *Discourses of Brigham Young* (DBY). Salt Lake City: Deseret Book, 1961.

ADAM

*W*hen our father Adam came into the garden of Eden, he came into it with a celestial body, and brought Eve, one of his wives, with him. He helped to make and organize this world. He is Michael, the Arch-angel, the Ancient of Days.—*JD, 1:50*

The Father frequently came to visit his son Adam, and talked and walked with him; and the children of Adam were more or less acquainted with him, and the things that pertain to God and to heaven were as familiar among mankind in the first ages of their existence on the earth as these mountains are to our mountain boys.—*DBY, 104*

And the Lord administered comfort unto Adam, and said unto him; I have set thee to be at the head—a multitude of nations shall come of thee, and thou art a prince over them forever . . .—*JD 10:355*

AGENCY

*B*ut," says the Father, ". . . I give each and every individual his agency; all must use that in order to gain exaltation in my kingdom; inasmuch as they have the power of choice they must exercise that power. They are my children; the attributes which you see in me are in my children and they must use their agency. If you undertake to save all, you must save them in unrighteousness and corruption."—*DBY, 53-54*

All rational beings have an agency of their own; and according to their own choice they will be damned or saved.—*JD, 6:97*

We cannot do all we please, because a great many times we want to and cannot, and that is what produces misery, which we call hell.—*JD, 13:33*

While we are governed and controlled by circumstances over which we have no power, still we possess ability and power in all our different spheres of action to call into existence circumstances to surround ourselves and our children, which will more or less control them; and, if they are planned in righteousness, will tend to lead us and our children to heaven.—*JD, 9:105*

Shall we not choose for ourselves? Yes. Have we not rights? Yes. Have we not power? Yes. Have we not authority bequeathed to us from the heavens—a legacy from God to hold dominion over the elements? Yes. Then go to like men—like angels—like Him we read of—whom we love and serve and worship.—*JD, 9:107*

AMERICA

his is the land that was given to Joseph—
the son so well beloved by his father Jacob;
and no king will ever reign upon it but the King,
the Lord. . . . God led our fathers from Europe to
this land, and prepared the way to break the yoke
that bound them, and inspired the guaranteed
freedom in our government, though that guarantee
is too often disregarded. He could bring forth his
work, and has prepared a people to receive and
commence his kingdom. Could this be done
anywhere else? No. He has known from the beginning of creation that this is the land whereon to
build this Zion.—*JD, 8:67*

The Lord has been operating for centuries to prepare the way for the coming forth of the contents of that Book from the bowels of the earth . . . It was the Lord who directed the discovery of this land to the nations of the old world, and its settlement, and the war for independence, and the final victory of the colonies, and the unprecedented prosperity of the American nation up to the calling of Joseph the Prophet. The Lord has dictated and directed the whole of this, for the bringing forth of his Kingdom in the last days.—*JD, 11:17*

ANGELS

*A*ll people have their guardian angels. Whether our departed dead guard us is not for me to say. I can say we have our guardian angels.—*JD, 13:76*

All the difference between men and angels is, men are passing through the day of trial that angels have already passed through. They belong to the same family that we do; but they have proven themselves worthy only of an exaltation to the state of angels, whereas we have the privilege of obtaining not only the same exaltation they enjoy, but of going further until we become Gods, even the sons of God.—*JD, 9:102-03*

When an angel is appointed to perform a duty, to go to the earth to preach the gospel, or to do anything for the advancement of his Father's kingdom in any part of the great domain of heaven, the vision of that angel is opened to see and understand the magnitude of the work that is expected of him to perform, and the grand results which will grow out of it. That is the reason why the angels are of one heart and of one mind, in their faithfulness and obedience to the requirements of their Father and God.—*JD, 11:15*

ANGER

I say, suffer not anger to rise in your countenance, to speak through your eyes, nor through your organs of speech, and in this way keep it down until you are free from it, as you would any other evil.—*JD, 10:175*

If the Devil says you cannot pray when you are angry, tell him it is none of his business—and pray until that species of insanity is dispelled and serenity is restored to the mind.—*JD, 10:175*

If you give way to your angry feelings . . . if you let your tongue run, it scatters the poison that is in you, and sets the whole being on fire. If you keep silent, you can master your feelings, can subdue your passions, and ultimately become masters of them and banish them from you.—*JD, 6:74-75*

Cease your anger, and sullenness of temper, and serve the Lord with cheerfulness, and singleness of heart.—*JD, 1:245*

Do not get so angry that you cannot pray: do not allow yourselves to become so angry that you cannot feed an enemy—even your worst enemy, if an opportunity should present itself. There is a wicked anger—and there is a righteous anger. The Lord does not suffer wicked anger to be in his heart.—*JD, 5:228-29*

APOSTLES

You cannot fill the office of a prophet, seer and revelator: God must do that . . . The Twelve are appointed by the finger of God. Here is Brigham, have his knees ever faltered? Have his lips ever quivered? Here is Heber and the rest of the Twelve, an independent body who have the keys of the priesthood—the keys of the kingdom of God to deliver to all the world: this is true, so help me God!—*McCloud, 128*

Joseph has conferred upon the heads of the Twelve all the keys and powers belonging to the Apostleship, and no man or set of men can get between Joseph and the Twelve in this world or in the world to come.—*Gates/Widtsoe, 42*

Now, brethren, the calling of an apostle is to build up the kingdom of God in all the world. If an apostle magnifies his calling, he is the word of the Lord to this people all the time—if he magnifies his calling, his words are the words of eternal life and salvation to those who hearken to them, just as much so as any written revelations.—*JD, 6:282*

ATONEMENT

*A*ll nations are going to share in these blessings; all are incorporated in the redemption of the Savior. He has tasted death for every man; they are all in his power, and he saves them all, as he says, except the sons of perdition; and the Father has put all the creations of this earth in his power. The earth itself, and mankind upon it, the brute beasts, the fish of the sea, and the fowls of heaven, the insects, and every creeping thing, with all things pertaining to this earthly ball—all are in the hands of the Savior, and he has redeemed them all.—*DBY, 388*

Sin is upon every earth that ever was created . . . consequently every earth has its redeemer, and every earth has its tempter; and every earth, and the people thereof, in their turn and time, receive all that we receive, and pass through all the ordeals that we are passing through.—*JD, 14:71-72*

This was no miracle to him. He had the issues of life and death in his power; he had power to lay down his life and the power to take it up again. This is what he says, and we must believe this if we believe the history of the Savior and the sayings of the Apostles recorded in the New Testament. Jesus had this power in and of himself; the Father bequeathed it to him; it was his legacy, and he had the power to lay down his life and take it again.—*DBY, 340-41*

To be Saints indeed requires every wrong influence that is within them, as individuals, to be subdued, until every evil desire is eradicated, and every feeling of the heart is brought into subjection to the will of Christ.—*JD, 19:66*

It requires all the atonement of Christ—the mercy of the Father—the pity of angels—and the grace of the Lord Jesus Christ to be with us always—and then to do the very best we possibly can, to get rid of this sin within us, so that we may escape from this world into the celestial kingdom.—*DBY, 60*

BAPTISM

*O*bedience to the ordinance of baptism is required that people may receive the remission of their sins . . . No man or woman ever received the faith of this Gospel but what desired to be baptized by immersion, and to have hands laid upon them for the Holy Ghost. Then come the blessings of healing, faith, prophecy, tongues, and so forth.—*JD, 14:96-7*

Who is there can say baptism is not necessary for the remission of sins? Jesus and the Apostles said it was necessary . . . and it is a fact that all who receive eternal life and salvation will receive it on no other conditions than believing in the Son of God and obeying the principles that he has laid down.—*JD, 13:213*

I did not know, when I was baptized, whether my wife believed the Gospel or not; I did not know that my father's house would go with me. I believed that some of them would (some already had), but I was brought to the test, "Can I forsake all for the Gospel's sake?" "I can," was the reply within me. "Would you like to?" "Yes, if they will not embrace the Gospel." "Will not these earthly, natural ties be continually in your bosom?" "No; I know no other family but the family of God gathered together, or about to be, in this my day; I have no other connection on the face of the earth that I claim."—*Arrington, 29*

Has water, in itself, any virtue to wash away sin? Certainly not, but the Lord says, 'If the sinner will repent of his sins, and go down into the waters of baptism, and there be buried in the likeness of being put into the earth and buried, and again be delivered from the water, in the likeness of being born—if in the sincerity of his heart he will do this, his sins shall be washed away.' Will the water of itself wash them away? No; but the keeping of the commandments of God will cleanse away the stain of sin.—*JD, 2:4*

BEAUTY

*G*od is the Supreme Architect. We owe all our inspiration, our love of beauty and the knowledge of how to express our views to the Father in Heaven who gives to His children what they ask for and what they need.—*McCloud, 266*

Beautify your gardens, your houses, your farms; beautify the city. This will make us happy, and produce plenty. The earth is a good earth, the elements are good if we will use them for our own benefit, in truth and righteousness. Then let us be content, and go to with our mights to make ourselves healthy, wealthy, and beautiful, and preserve ourselves in the best possible manner, and live just as long as we can, and do all the good we can.—*JD, 15:20*

BIBLE

*T*he Book of Mormon declares that the Bible is true, and it proves it; and the two prove each other true.—*JD, 13:175*

. . . The reading of the Bible gives comfort and happiness to the traveler to eternity, and points out to him in part the character and attributes of the Being whom to know is life eternal.—*JD, 7:332*

I believe that the Bible contains the word of God, and the words of good men and the words of bad men; . . . but aside from that I believe the doctrines concerning salvation contained in that book are true, and that their observance will elevate any people, nation or family that dwells on the face of the earth.—*JD, 13:175*

It is your privilege and duty to live so as to be able to understand the things of God. There are the

27

Old and New Testaments, the Book of Mormon, and the book of Doctrine and Covenants, which Joseph has given us, and they are of great worth to a person wandering in darkness. They are like a lighthouse in the ocean, or a finger-post which points out the road we should travel. Where do they point? To the Fountain of light.—*DBY, 127*

BISHOPS

*I*n the capacity of a Bishop, has any person a right to direct the spiritual affairs of the kingdom of God? No. In that capacity his right is restricted to affairs of a temporal and moral point of view. He has a right to deal with the transgressor . . . A Bishop can try a man for a breach of moral conduct, but he cannot sit in judgment on contro-verted points of doctrine, for they are to be referred to those who hold the keys of the higher Priesthood, and their decision is the end to all strife.—*JD, 9:91*

If you suffer yourselves to find fault with your Bishop, you condescend to the spirit of apostasy. Do any of you do this? If you do, you do not realize that you expose yourself to the power of the Enemy. What should your faith and position be before God? Such that, if a Bishop does not do right, the Lord will remove him out of your Ward. You are not to find fault.—*JD, 9:141*

Take a man of the weakest intellect of any in a Ward and ordain him a Bishop, and then let every other man in that Ward be filled with the power of his holy calling . . . their faith is concentrated upon him; they pray for him early and late, that the Lord will fill him with wisdom, enlarge his understanding, open the visions of his mind, and show him things as they are in time and in eternity. You all know that even such a man would become mighty in the house of Israel, if he had the faith of his Ward.—*JD, 7:278*

BLESSINGS

*S*o long as any people live up to the best light they have, the Almighty will multiply blessings upon them by blessing the earth and causing it to bring forth in its strength, to fill their storehouses with plenty.—*JD, 9:169*

If the Lord had a people on the earth that he had perfect confidence in, there is not a blessing in the eternities of our God, that they could not bear in the flesh, that he would not pour out upon them. Tongue cannot tell the blessings the Lord has for a people who have proved themselves before him.—*JD, 4:79*

The greatest blessing that can be bestowed on the children of men is power to civilize themselves after the order of the civilization of the heavens—to prepare themselves to dwell with heavenly beings who are capable of enduring the presence of the Gods.—*DBY, 455*

Book of Mormon

I weighed the matter studiously for nearly two years before I made up my mind to receive that Book. I looked at it on all sides. All other religions I could fathom…but this new one I reasoned on month after month, until I came to a certain knowledge of its truth. Had this not been the case I never would have embraced it to this day. I wished time sufficient to prove all things for myself.—McCloud, 36

The Lord has been operating for centuries to prepare the way for the coming forth of the contents of the Book of Mormon from the bowels of the earth, to be published to the world, to show to the inhabitants thereof that he still lives, and that he will, in the latter days, gather his elect from the four corners of the earth. . . — *DBY, 109*

How many witnesses has the Book of Mormon? Hundreds and thousands are now living upon the earth, who testify to its truth.—*JD, 10:326*

CELESTIAL KINGDOM, GLORY

*W*e read in the Bible that there is one glory of the sun, another glory of the moon, and another glory of the stars. . . . These are worlds, different departments, or mansions, in our Father's house. Now those men, or those women, who know no more about the power of God, and the influences of the Holy Spirit, than to be led entirely by another person, suspending their own understanding, and pinning their faith upon another's sleeve, will never be capable of entering into the celestial glory, to be crowned as they anticipate; they will never be capable of becoming Gods . . . Who will? Those who are valiant and inspired with the true independence of heaven, who will go forth boldly in the service of their God, leaving others to do as they please, determined to do right, though all mankind besides should take the opposite course.—*JD, 1:312*

All heaven is anxious that the people should be saved. The heavens weep over the people, because of their hard-heartedness, unbelief, and slowness to believe and act.—*DBY, 388-89*

The kingdom that this people are in pertains to the Celestial kingdom; it is a kingdom in which we can prepare to go into the presence of the Father and the Son. Then let us live to inherit that glory. God has promised you, Jesus has promised you, and the apostles and prophets of old and of our day have promised you that you shall be rewarded according to all you can desire in righteousness before the Lord, if you live for that reward.—*DNW, 31 Oct. 1860, 1*

I have now told you what course to pursue to obtain an exaltation. The Lord must be first and foremost in our affections; the building up of his cause and kingdom demands our first consideration.—*DNW, 5 Jan. 1854, 2*

CHARACTER

*I*f you were in possession of all the wealth in the world, it is not worth so much to you as your good characters. Preserve them. If you have a happy influence with your brethren and sisters, preserve it, for it is more choice than fine gold.—*JD, 8:346*

You breathe one breath at a time; each moment is set apart to its act, and each act to its moment. It is the moments and the little acts that make the sum of the life of man. Let every second, minute, hour, and day we live be spent in doing that which we know to be right.—*JD, 3:342*

The name of king or emperor has always sunk into insignificance when I contrasted it with the character of a man of God—of a person who holds the destinies of men in his hands, and can dispense them to the people. Such a man should preserve himself like a God, or an angel of God.—*JD, 8:347*

There is one duty we owe to ourselves and to our fellow men, it is to never abuse the confidence others may place in us, or by our folly or criminality break down the character we have built up by a life of industry and honesty. Our character is not entirely our individual property; it belongs partly to our neighbors, and we have no right to shake their confidence in us and in mankind generally by acts inconsistent with the good name we have established.—*Jesse, 228*

CHARITY

Only a few men on the earth understand the charity that fills the bosom of our Savior. We should have charity; we should do all we can to reclaim the lost sons and daughters of Adam and Eve, and bring them back to be saved in the presence of our Father and God. If we do this, our charity will extend to the utmost extent that it is designed for the charity of God to extend in the midst of this people.—*DBY, 273*

The genius of our religion is to have mercy upon all, do good to all, as far as they will let us do good to them.—*JD, 11:282*

Respect one another; do not speak lightly of each other. Some, if they get a little pique against an individual, are disposed to cast him down to hell, as not worthy of a place upon earth. O fools! Not to understand that those you condemn are the workmanship of God, as well as yourselves! God overlooks their weaknesses; and so far as they do good, they are as acceptable as we are. Thank God that you know better, and be full of mercy and kindness.—*DBY, 274*

God bless the humble and the righteous, and may He have compassion upon us because of the weakness that is in our nature. And considering the great weakness and ignorance of mortals—let us have mercy upon each other.—*McCloud, 299*

CHASTITY

Every virtuous woman desires a husband to whom she can look for guidance and protection through this world. God has placed this desire in woman's nature. It should be respected by the stronger sex. Any man who takes advantage of this, and humbles a daughter of Eve, to rob her of her virtue, and cast her off dishonored and defiled, is her destroyer, and is responsible to God for the deed. If the refined Christian society of the nineteenth century will tolerate such a crime, God will not; but he will call the perpetrator to an account.—*JD, 11:268*

I will promise every man on the face of this earth, that ever was or ever will be, that if they will betray the innocent and ruin the virtuous they shall have damnation for their portion.—*JD, 11:289*

CHILDREN

*N*ever allow yourselves to become out of temper and get fretful. "Why," mother says, "this is a very mischievous little boy or girl." What do you see? That amount of vitality in those little children that they cannot be still…They are so full of life…that their bones fairly ache with strength…and activity…Do not be out of temper yourselves. Always sympathize with them and soothe them. Be mild and pleasant.—*Arrington, 332.*

Solomon said, "He that spareth his rod hateth his son," but instead of using the rod, I will teach my children by example and by precept. I will teach them every opportunity I have to cherish faith, to exercise patience, to be full of long-suffering and kindness. It is not by the whip or the rod that we make obedient children; but it is by faith and by prayer, and by setting a good example before them.—*JD, 11:117*

Now, children, remember this. We teach you that our Father in heaven is a personage of tabernacle, just as much as I am who stand before you today . . . and he loves you, and knows you, for you are all his offspring . . . this is the kind of God we worship. Children, call upon him in your childhood and youth, for from such as you he has said he will not turn away. Ask the Father to protect you . . . cease not to call upon God with all your hearts. Remember this. Obey your parents, honor them and seek to do them good.—*JD, 19: 64,65*

Many of the sisters grieve because they are not blessed with offspring . . . Be faithful, and if you are not blessed with children in this time, you will be hereafter . . . You will see the time when you will have millions of children around you. If you are faithful to your covenants, you will be mothers of nations.—*JD, 8:203*

When the Lord suffers children of all ages to be taken from us, it is for our good, and for theirs . . . it is consoling to think that, when our children are taken from the earth in their infancy, they are safe . . . It gives me great joy to understand that every child that has been taken from this mortality to the spiritual world, from the day mother Eve bore her first child to this time, is an heir to the celestial kingdom and glory of God.—*JD, 10:366-67*

If children knew the feelings of their parents when they did good or evil, it would have a salutary influence upon their lives; but no child can possibly know this, until it becomes a parent. I am compassionate therefore toward children.— *Arrington, 332*

I say to all, God bless you, my children, my little ones. I am a great lover of children and innocence and purity.—JD, 19:65

CHRIST

*J*esus is the first begotten from the dead, as you will understand. Neither Enoch, Elijah, Moses, nor any other man that ever lived on earth, no matter how strictly he lived, ever obtained a resurrection until after Jesus Christ's body was called from the tomb by the angel. He was the first begotten from the dead. He is the Master of the resurrection.—*DBY, 374*

The Spirit of the Lord enlightens every man that comes into the world. There is no one that lives upon the earth but what is, more or less, enlightened by the Spirit of the Lord Jesus. It is said of him, that he is the light of the world. He lighteth every man that comes into the world and every person, at times, has the light of the spirit of truth upon him.—*DBY, 32*

He [Christ] wrought miracles and performed a good work on the earth; but of himself he did nothing. Do you not all firmly believe that the whole soul, heart, reflections, thoughts, and all the being of the Son of God were operated upon and did show forth that all he did manifest and bring forth pertaining to his mission was according to the word and will of his Father? Certainly you do.—*JD, 6:96*

I will take the liberty of saying to every man and woman who wishes to obtain salvation through him (the Savior), that looking to him, only, is not enough: they must have faith in his name, character and atonement; and they must have faith in his father and in the plan of salvation devised and wrought out by the Father and the Son. What will this faith lead to? It will lead to obedience to the requirements of the Gospel.—*JD, 13:56*

This people must be pure in heart . . . The greatest and most important of all the requirements of our Father in heaven . . . is to believe in Jesus Christ, confess him, seek to him, cling to him, make friends with him. Take a course to open and keep open a communication with your Elder Brother.—*JD, 8:339*

What earthly power can gather a people as this people have been gathered, and hold them together as this people have been held together? It was not Joseph, it is not Brigham, nor Heber, nor any of the rest of the Twelve . . . but it is the Lord God Almighty that holds this people together, and no other power.—*McCloud, 296-97*

CONSECRATION

To whom do these elements belong? To the same Being who owned them in the beginning. The earth is still His, and its fulness, and that includes each one of us, and includes all that we seem to possess. . . . The ability which we have to bring them together we have received of the Lord, by His free gift, and He has made us capable of performing many things for His glory, for His wisdom, and for the exaltation of those creatures He has brought forth and made.—*JD, 2:300*

I have nothing, only what the Lord has put in my possession. It is his; I am his, and all I ask is for him to tell me what to do with my time, my talents and the means that he puts in my possession. It is to be devoted to his kingdom. Let every other man and woman do the same, and all the surplus we make is in one great amount for accomplishing the purposes of the Lord. He says,

44

"I will make you the richest people on the earth." Now, go to work, Latter-day Saints, and make yourselves one, and all needed blessings will follow.—*JD, 17:54*

I speak unto those who are inclined to love the substance of this world better than the Lord. If you have gold and silver, let it not come between you and your duty . . . what hinders this people from being as holy as the Church of Enoch? . . . It is because you will not cultivate the disposition to be so! . . . Were we to dedicate our moral and intellectual influence, and our earthly wealth to the Lord, our hearts would be very likely to applaud our acts.—*JD, 1:202*

CONTENTION

*Y*ou see, hear and witness a good deal of contention among the children—some of you do, if not all—and I will give you a few words with regard to your future lives, that you may have children that are not contentious, not quarrelsome. Always be good-natured yourselves, is the first step. Never allow yourselves to become out of temper and get fretful . . . They [children] have so much vitality in them that their bones fairly ache with strength. They have such an amount of vitality—life, strength and activity, that they must dispose of them; and the young ones will contend with each other. Do not be out of temper yourselves. Always sympathize with them and soothe them. Be mild and pleasant.—*JD, 19:69*

I consider it a disgrace to the community, and in the eyes of the Lord, and of angels, and in the eyes of all the Prophets and Revelators that have ever lived upon the earth, when a community will descend to a low, degraded state of contention with each other.—*JD, 1:32*

A perfect oneness will save a people, because intelligent beings cannot become perfectly one, only by acting upon principles that pertain to eternal life. Wicked men may be partially united in evil; but, in the very nature of things, such a union is of short duration. The very principle upon which they are partially united will itself breed contention and disunion to destroy the temporary compact. Only the line of truth and righteousness can secure to any kingdom or people, either of earthly or heavenly existence, an eternal continuation of perfect union; for only truth and those who are sanctified by it can dwell in celestial glory.—*JD, 7:277*

CONSTITUTION

*W*e mean to sustain the Constitution of the United States and all righteous laws.—*DBY, 358*

We will cling to the Constitution of our country, and to the government that reveres that sacred charter of freemen's rights; and, if necessary, pour out our best blood for the defense of every good and righteous principle.—*DBY, 358*

To accuse us of being unfriendly to the Government, is to accuse us of hostility to our religion, for no item of inspiration is held more sacred with us than the Constitution under which she acts. As a religious society, we, in common with all other denominations, claim its protection.—*DBY, 359*

When the day comes in which the Kingdom of God will bear rule, the flag of the United States will proudly flutter unsullied on the flagstaff of liberty and equal rights, without a spot to sully its fair surface; the glorious flag our fathers have bequeathed to us will then be unfurled to the breeze by those who have power to hoist it aloft and defend its sanctity.—*DBY, 360*

When the Constitution of the United States hangs, as it were, upon a single thread, they will have to call for the "Mormon" Elders to save it from utter destruction; and they will step forth and do it.—*DBY, 361*

The present Constitution, with a few alterations of a trifling nature, is just as good as we want; and if it is sustained on this land of Joseph, it will be done by us and our posterity.—*DBY, 361*

COVENANTS

here is not a man or woman, who violates the covenants made with their God, that will not be required to pay the debt. The blood of Christ will never wipe that out, your own blood must atone for it; and the judgments of the Almighty will come, sooner or later, and every man and woman will have to atone for breaking their covenants. To what degree? Will they have to go to hell? They are in hell enough now. I do not wish them in a greater hell, when their consciences condemn them all the time. Let compassion reign in our bosoms. Try to comprehend how weak we are, how we are organized, how the spirit and the flesh are continually at war.—*JD, 3:247*

It is a sign which you make in token of your covenant with God and with one another, and it is for you to perform your vows. When you raise your hands to heaven and let them fall and then pass on with your covenants unfulfilled, you will be cursed.—*DBY, 396*

I feel sometimes like lecturing men and women severely who enter into covenants without realizing the nature of the covenants they make, and who use little or no effort to fulfill them.—*DBY, 396*

It is one of the greatest blessings we could enjoy, to come before the Lord, and before the angels, and before each other, to witness that we remember that the Lord Jesus Christ has died for us. This proves to the Father that we remember our covenants, that we love his Gospel, that we love to keep his commandments, and to honor the name of the lord Jesus upon the earth.—*JD, 6:277*

Many of the sisters grieve because they are not blessed with offspring. You will see the time when you will have millions of children around you. If you are faithful to your covenants, you will be mothers of nations.—*JD, 8:208*

COVETOUSNESS

I am more afraid of covetousness in our Elders than I am of the hordes of hell. Have we men out now of that class? I believe so . . . All our enemies in the United States or in the world, and all hell with them marshaled against us, could not do us the injury that covetousness in the hearts of this people could do us; for it is idolatry.—*JD, 5:353*

The great stumbling block in the midst of this people is, that their minds are not yet wholly weaned from the evil habits and practices of the world. With some, the end of strife and covetousness has not yet come . . . we must gain the spiritual victory . . . before we can have the privilege of proclaiming the building up of the people of God.—*JD, 5:329*

Those who are covetous and greedy, anxious to grasp the whole world, are all the time uneasy, and are constantly laying their plans and contriving how to obtain this, that, and the other ... How the Devil will play with a man who so worships gain!—*DBY, 306*

Men are greedy for the vain things of this world. In their hearts they are covetous. It is true that the things of this world are designed to make us comfortable, and they make some people as happy as they can be here; but riches can never make the Latter-day Saints happy. Riches of themselves can not produce permanent happiness; only the Spirit that comes from above can do that.—*DBY, 306*

CREATION

*T*he whole object of the creation of this world is to exalt the intelligences that are placed upon it, that they may live, endure, and increase for ever and ever.—DBY, 57

Things were first created spiritually; the Father actually begat the spirits, and they were brought forth and lived with Him. Then He commenced the work of creating earthly tabernacles, precisely as He had been created in the flesh himself, by partaking of the coarse material that was organized and composed this earth, until His system was charged with it, consequently the tabernacles of His children were organized from the coarse materials of this earth.—JD, 4:218

I suppose that God never organized an earth and peopled it that was ever reduced to a lower state of darkness, sin and ignorance than this. I suppose this is one of the lowest kingdoms that ever the Lord Almighty created, and on that account is capable of becoming exalted to be one of the highest kingdoms that has ever had an exaltation in all the eternities. In proportion as it has been reduced—so will it be exalted, with that portion of its inhabitants who, in their humiliation, have cleaved to righteousness and acknowledged God in all things.—JD, 10:175

DANCE

*T*he world considers it very wicked for a Christian to hear music and to dance. Many preachers say that fiddling and music come from hell; but I say there is no fiddling, there is no music in hell. Music belongs to heaven, to cheer God, angels and men. If we could hear the music there is in heaven, it would overwhelm us mortals. Music and dancing are for the benefit of holy ones, and all of those who come here to-night who are not holy and righteous and do not worship God have no right to be here.—*Gates/Widtsoe, 81-82*

I want it distinctly understood, that fiddling and dancing are no part of our worship. What are they for then?…That my body may keep pace with my mind. My mind labors like a man logging, all the time; and this is the reason why I am fond of these pastimes—they give me a privilege to throw everything off, and shake myself, that my body may exercise, and my mind rest.—*JD, 1:30*

As the pressure of persecution increased, the temple seemed the only place of refuge left the Saints. On more than one occasion they gathered there to praise the Lord in song and dance, enjoying the sweet fellowship such activities offered. "The spirit of dancing increased," Brigham wrote, "until the whole floor was covered with dancers, and while we danced before the Lord, we shook the dust from off our feet as a testimony against this nation."—*McCloud, 136*

DAY OF REST

(See Sabbath)

DEATH

No person who believes on the Lord Jesus Christ has a right to spend a day, an hour, or a minute of his life or her life in a manner unbecoming the profession of a Saint; they should be ready to depart this life any moment.—*JD, 17:140*

When shall we die? Never. Says our Savior, "Whosoever believeth in me shall never die." Shall we put on this mortality? Yes, we will lay down these bodies in the grave. What for? That the dust, our mother earth, that composes the house of the spirit, may be purified by passing through this ordeal, and be prepared to be called up and united with the intelligent heavenly body that God has prepared. This is nothing but a change. It is not the dissolution of the creature; it is merely putting off the flesh that pertains to this world.—*JD, 8:43*

We are naturally inclined to cling to our mother earth; our bodies love to live here, to see, to hear, to breathe, and to enjoy themselves, because we are of the earth, earthy. But probably, in most cases, the change from mortal to immortality is no greater, comparatively speaking, than when a child emerges into this world. We shall suffer no more in putting off this flesh and leaving the spirit houseless than the child, in its capacity, does in its first efforts to breathe the breath of this mortal life.—*JD, 8:28*

To me life is increase, death is the opposite . . . if mankind will choose the opposite to life held out in the Gospel, it will lead them to dissolution, to decomposition, to death . . but to simply take the path pointed out in the Gospel, by those who have given us the plan of salvation, is to take the path that leads to life, to eternal increase; it is to pursue that course where we shall never, never lose what we obtain, but continue to collect, to gather together, to increase, to spread abroad and extend to an endless duration.—*JD, 1:350*

Those who have honored their calling and Priesthood to the end die in the Lord, and their works do follow them. . . It is a matter of rejoicing more than the day of birth . . . it is true it is grievous to part with our friends. We are creatures of passion, of sympathy, of love, and it is painful for us to part with our friends . . . But we have joy in the dissolution of the body . . . That silent clay is consigned to rest, and the spirit is free—gone to God who gave it.—*JD,:13:75-76*

DEBT

A man who will not pay his honest debts is no Latter-day Saint, if he has the means to pay them. A man who will run into debt, when he has no prospect of paying it back again, does not understand the principles that should prevail . . . —*JD, 11:258*

It is bad enough, quite bad enough, to borrow from an enemy and not to repay him; to do this is beneath the character of any human being; but all who will borrow from a friend, and especially from the poor, are undeserving the fellowship of the Saints if they do not repay.—*DBY, 304*

DEVIL

(See Satan)

DUTY

*I*t is the duty of every Latter-day Saint, young or old, to serve the Lord. None of us are excused from this duty as, also, none of us are shut out from the attainment of the blessings of eternal life. Never in all your associations forget that you are a Latter-day Saint . . . never be ashamed to do what is right.—*Jessee, 302*

It was asked me by a gentleman how I guided the people by revelation. I teach them to so live that the Spirit of revelation may make plain to them their duty day by day that they are able to guide themselves.—*McCloud, 283*

You will find that much of the happiness of this life consists in having something worthy to do and in doing it well . . . No one advances who imagines himself too good or too big for present duties. Such a one is apt to sink into a smaller and a smaller place. In the long run, and for the most part, men are found in the places they have fitted themselves to fill.—*Jessee, 305-06*

Take a course to open and keep a communication with your Elder Brother or file-leader—our Savior. Were I to draw a distinction in all the duties that are required of the children of men, from first to last, I would place first and foremost the duty of seeking unto the Lord our God until we open the path of communication from heaven to earth—from God to our own souls.—*McCloud, 297*

EVE

When Father Adam came to assist in organizing the earth out of the crude material that was found, an earth was made upon which the children of men could live. After the earth was prepared Father Adam came and stayed here, and there was a woman brought to him. There was a certain woman brought to Father Adam whose name was Eve, because she was the first woman, and she was given to him to be his wife.—*DBY, 102*

We all belong to the races which have sprung from Father Adam and Mother Eve; and every son and daughter of that God we serve, who organized this earth and millions of others, and who holds them in existence by law.—*DBY, 105*

The Devil had truth in his mouth as well as lies when he came to Mother Eve. Said he, "If you will eat of the fruit of the tree of knowledge of good and evil, you will see as God sees." That was just as true as anything that ever was spoken on the face of the earth. She did eat, her eyes were opened, and she saw good and evil.—*JD, 12:70*

Some may regret that our first parents sinned. This is nonsense. If we had been there, and they had not sinned, we should have sinned. I will not blame Adam or Eve. Why? Because it was necessary that sin should enter the world.—*DBY, 103*

EVIL

*D*o not trifle with evil, or you will be overcome by it before you know. Our business is to build up the Zion of God on the earth. Do you think you will do it and go hand in hand with the wicked? No.—*JD, 12:231*

We have a warfare. As the Apostle says, "For we wrestle not against flesh and blood, but against principalities and against powers, against the rulers of the darkness of this world, against spiritual wickedness in high places." This warfare commences within us.—*JD, 10:105*

Through the Fall, we have partaken so much of the nature of the enemy—he has so much influence in the flesh of every person, that we have to summon all our force and to use every effort to propel our bark up stream, or to put down iniquity in our own hearts and inclinations.—*JD, 14:194*

Reason as to why it is that you can remember an injury better than a kindness; why you can retain hatred longer than love . . . is it rather because the power of the tempter has control over you, and because the world is full of evil principles, and you have adhered to them? Yes, this is the cause, and you must acknowledge it. The whole world is contaminated with a spirit to remember evil and forget the good.—*JD, 3:356*

But whence comes evil? It comes when we make an evil of a good.—*JD, 8:341*

If you feel evil, keep it to yourselves until you overcome that evil principle. This is what I call resisting the devil, and he flees from me. I strive to not speak evil, to not feel evil, and if I do, to keep it to myself until it is gone from me, and not let it pass my lips.—*JD, 3:195*

None of us are so strong in well doing that we can afford to associate with the depraved, keep company with the dissolute, and pick out our friends from amongst those who love sin and delight in iniquity. It is a mockery to pray to God to "leave us not in temptation," and then seek the companionship of the tempter. However strong in the Lord men may feel, it is always the wisest policy to drive as far as possible from the precipices of sin.—*Jessee, 227*

When truth comes, error comes also. The good spirit tries to overcome the wayward will of the flesh, and the flesh, aided by the cunning and power of the devil, maintains a strong warfare; but notwithstanding this great power against which the spirit has to contend, the power of God is greater than the power of the wicked one.—*JD, 11:237*

It is the evil that people do which renders them obnoxious to the heavens, hateful to each other, and unworthy of their being upon the earth.—*JD, 12:210*

EXALTATION (OR ETERNAL SALVATION)

*L*et the people be led by the revelations of Jesus Christ, and the finger of God will be made manifest before them day by day in their progress to eternal happiness; for this is the privilege of the faithful.—*JD, 9:107*

I expect, if I am faithful with yourselves, that I shall see the time with yourselves that we shall know how to prepare to organize an earth like this—know how to people that earth, how to redeem it, how to sanctify it, and how to glorify it, with those who live upon it who will hearken to our counsels. The Father and the Son have attained to this point already; I am on the way, and so are you, and every faithful servant of God.—*JD, 6:274-75*

This intelligence must endure . . . The glory and intelligence that God has prepared for the faithful, no man knoweth. Should not this fill every heart with peace and joy—that there is no end to the progress of knowledge?—*JD, 8:155*

We have not yet received our kingdoms, neither will we, until we have finished our work on earth . . . Then he that has overcome and is found worthy, will be made a king of kings, a lord of lords over his own posterity, or in other words: A father of fathers.—*JD, 10:255*

To be damned is to be banished from, or be deprived of living in the presence of the Father and the Son. Who will live with him? They [who] will come up and inherit the highest glory that is prepared for the faithful.—*JD, 11:271*

All intelligent beings who are crowned with crowns of glory, immortality, and eternal lives must pass through every ordeal appointed for intelligent beings to pass through, to gain their glory and exaltation. Every calamity that can come upon mortal beings will be suffered to come upon the few, to prepare them to enjoy the presence of the Lord . . . Every trial and experience you have passed through is necessary for your salvation.—*McCloud, 66*

FAITH

*I*f we speak of faith in the abstract, it is the power of God by which the worlds are and were made, and is a gift of God to those who believe and obey his commandments.—*JD, 8:259*

I have faith in my God, and that faith corresponds with the works I produce. I have no confidence in faith without works.—*JD, 4:24*

My faith is, when we have done all we can, then the Lord is under obligation, and will not disappoint the faithful; he will perform the rest.—*McCloud, 42*

The Gospel that we preach is the power of God unto salvation; and the first principle of that Gospel is, faith in God, and faith in Jesus Christ, his Son, our Savior.—*DBY, 153*

It is the easiest thing in the world to believe the truth. It is a great deal easier to believe truth than error. It is easier to defend truth than to defend error.—*JD, 19:42*

When you believe the principles of the Gospel and attain unto faith, which is a gift of God, he adds more faith, adding faith to faith. He bestows faith upon his creatures as a gift.—*JD, 8:17*

If the people will only be full of good works, I will insure that they will have faith in time of need.—*JD, 3:154*

When faith springs up in the heart, good works follow, and good works will increase that pure faith within them.—*JD, 3:155*

We have come here to build up Zion. How shall we do it? I have told you a great many times . . . We should go to work with a united faith like the heart of one man; and whatsoever we do should be performed in the name of the Lord, and we will then be blessed and prospered in all we do. We have a work on hand whose magnitude can hardly be told.—*McCloud, 299*

If there is anything that gives joy to the hearts of the fathers in this kingdom it is the knowledge that their sons seize the holy principles for which they have so long labored in the name of Jesus, and that their children are preparing themselves by faith and good works to bear off the kingdom triumphant.—*Jessee 135*

If the Latter-day Saints will walk up to their privileges, and exercise faith in the name of Jesus Christ, and live in the enjoyment of the fulness of the Holy Ghost constantly day by day, there is nothing on the face of the earth that they could ask for, that would not be given them. The Lord is waiting to be very gracious unto this people.—*DBY, 156*

FAMILY

*T*here is not another community on the earth where families are loved, honored, respected and cherished as they are among the Latter-day Saints.—*JD, 11:289*

Do you want your children to be Saints when they are grown up?...Then lay the foundation for their future life by teaching each little child what it should do...Train that child by your own acts and words...Teach the children so that when they go out from the presence of their father and mother, God is in all their thoughts.—*JD, 19:71*

We must commence our labors of love and kindness with the family to which we belong; and then extend to others. . . . If we do not seek the welfare of the household of faith, we will sooner or later deny the faith.—*JD, 11:288*

You may well say to yourselves, "If I can do as well as my parents, I think I shall do well, and be as good as I want to be, and I should not strive to excel them." But if you do your duty you will far excel them in everything that is good—in holiness, in physical and intellectual strength, for this is your privilege, and it becomes your duty.—*JD, 2:18*

Fathers, mothers, brothers and sisters are no more to me than are other persons, unless they embrace this work. Here are my fathers, my mothers, my sisters and my brethren in the Kingdom, and I have none outside of it, neither in any part of the earth, nor in all the eternities of the Gods. In this Kingdom are my acquaintances, relatives, and friends—my soul, my affections, my all.—*DBY, 204*

FATHERS

The father should be full of kindness, and endeavor to happify and cheer the mother, that her heart may be comforted and her affections unimpaired in her earthly protector, that her love for God and righteousness may vibrate throughout her whole being.—*JD, 8:62*

It is for the husband to learn how to gather around his family the comforts of life, how to control his passions and temper, and how to command the respect, not only of his family but of all his brethren, sisters, and friends.—*DBY, 198*

At Sugar Creek, as Camp of Israel was being organized: "Ten a.m. I walked up the valley with Amasa Lyman and Willard Richards where we united in prayer . . . then returned to camp and continued the organization, acting the part of a father to everybody."—*McCloud, 140*

Susa on her father, Brigham: "Correct his children, he did, but each with that dignity and deliberation that neither humiliated the child nor lowered his own self-respect . . . brutal he could not be, firm he always was. But the corrected child, inheriting his own poise, subconsciously admitted the justice of the rebuke and was the first to fly for forgiveness to his fatherly bosom."—*Gates/Widtsoe, 355*

Let the father be the head of the family, the master of his own household; and let him treat them as an angel would treat them.—*JD, 4:55*

Susa: "Father was great in his handling of large affairs, in his infinite power to mold men and measures; but if he had failed, as he himself once said, in his duties as husband and father, he would have waked up in the morning of the First Resurrection to find he had failed in everything."—*Gates/Widtsoe, 340*

I want to tell you, each and every one of you, that you are well acquainted with God, our Heavenly Father, or the great Elohim. You are all well acquainted with him, for there is not a soul of you but what has lived in his house and dwelt with him year after year; and yet you are seeking to become acquainted with him, when the fact is, you have merely forgotten what you did know. There is not a person here to-day but what is a son or a daughter of that Being. In the spirit world their spirits were first begotten and brought forth, and they lived there with their parents for ages before they came here. This, perhaps, is hard for many to believe, but it is the greatest nonsense in the world not to believe it. If you do not believe it, cease to call him Father, and when you pray, pray to some other character.—*McCloud, 297-98*

FORGIVENESS

*D*o not throw away a man or a woman, old or young. If they commit an evil today and another tomorrow, but wish to be Saints and to be forgiven, do you forgive them, not only seven times, but seventy times seven in a day, if their hearts are fully set to do right. Let us make it a point to pass over their weaknesses and say, "God bless you in trying to be better in time to come," and act as wise stewards in the kingdom of God.—*JD, 8:368*

Put away all unkind feelings, and let all your meditations be correct . . . Avoid nursing misunderstandings into difficulties.—*JD, 8:72*

Let us have compassion upon each other, and let the strong tenderly nurse the weak into strength, and let those who can see guide the blind until they can see the way for themselves.—*DBY, 272*

A man or woman who has embraced, and who enjoys, the principles of this Church, ought to live like an angel. They ought never to be angry with each other, but live in the light of the truth continually, and every man be kind to his neighbor.—*JD, 1:245*

FREE AGENCY

(See Agency)

FREEDOM

*W*e believe that the Lord has been preparing that when he should bring forth his work that, when the time should fully come, there might be a place upon his footstool where sufficient liberty of conscience should exist, that his Saints might dwell in peace under the broad panoply of constitutional law and equal rights. In this view we consider that the men in the Revolution were inspired by the Almighty, to throw off the shackles of the mother government, with her established religion. For this cause were Adams, Jefferson, Franklin, Washington, and a host of others inspired to deeds of resistance to the acts of the King of Great Britain, who might also have been led to those aggressive acts, for aught we know, to bring to pass the purposes of God, in thus establishing a new government upon a principle of greater freedom, a basis of self-government allowing the free exercise of religious worship.— *DBY, 359-60*

There is no freedom anywhere outside the Gospel of salvation.—*JD, 5:52*

I say God speed everybody that is for freedom and equal rights! I am with you. Whom do we want to fill our public offices? We want the best men that we can find for governor, president and statesmen, and for every other office of trust and responsibility; and when we have obtained them, we will pray for them and give them our faith and influence to do the will of God and to preserve themselves and the people in truth and righteousness.—*JD, 13:274*

GATHERING OF ISRAEL

*I*t is the house of Israel we are after, and we care not whether they come from the east, the west, the north, or the south . . . if the Gentiles are grafted into the good olive tree they will partake of its root and fatness.—*JD, 2:269*

We are gathered together expressly to build up the kingdom of God. . . . The voice of God has not called us together from the uttermost parts of the earth to build up and enrich those who are diametrically opposed to His kingdom . . . No, we are gathered together to become of one heart and of one mind in all our operations and endeavors.—*JD, 12:153*

Ephraim has become mixed with all the nations of the earth, and it is Ephraim that is gathering together.—*DBY, 121*

What earthly power can gather a people as this people have been gathered, and hold them together as this people have been held together? It was not Joseph, it is not Brigham, nor Heber, nor any of the rest of the Twelve . . . but it is the Lord God Almighty who holds this people together, and no other power.—*McCloud, 224-25*

We are gathering the people as fast as we can. We are gathering them to make Saints of them and of ourselves.—*DBY, 121*

GIFTS

(See Spiritual Gifts)

GOD

*T*he Lord is more merciful to the people than we are . . . He has compassion on the works of his hands.—*JD, 14:149*

I wish the people to understand that they have no interest apart from the Lord our God. The moment you have a divided interest, that moment you sever yourselves from eternal principles."—*JD, 4:31*

To whom do these elements belong now? To the same Being who owned them in the beginning. The earth is still His, and its fulness, and that includes each one of us, and also includes all that we seem to possess.—*JD, 2:300*

Let every person be the friend of God.—*JD, 4:372*

We only ask favors of our God; and He is the Being we serve; to Him we go . . . We serve the living and true God . . . and the wicked may help themselves the best they can.—*McCloud, 126*

I do not wish men to understand that I had anything to do with our being moved here, that was the providence of the Almighty. It was the power of God that wrought out salvation for this people. I never could have devised such a plan.—*McCloud, 152*

He is our Heavenly Father; he is also our God, and the Maker and upholder of all things in heaven and on earth . . . he knoweth every thought and intent of the hearts of all living, for he is everywhere present by the power of his Spirit—his minister, the Holy Ghost. He is the Father of all, is above all, through all, and in you all; he knoweth all things pertaining to this earth, and he knows all things pertaining to millions of earths like this.—*DBY, 19*

Every true principle, every true science, every art, all knowledge that men possess, or that they ever did or ever will possess, is from God. We should take pains and pride to . . . rear our children so that the learning and education of the world may be theirs.—*McCloud, 270*

GOOD

*S*ome desire to do good all the time, still it seems that almost every act they perform results in evil; look upon such persons as they are, through eyes of mercy, and not measure them with your measure.—*JD, 10:175*

We are the teachers of life and salvation . . . all who do not want to sustain co-operation and fall into the ranks of improvement, and endeavor to improve themselves by every good book and then by every principle that has been received from heaven, had better go back . . . we do not care where you go, if you will only go.—*JD, 13:4*

The Gospel of the Son of God is the only thing that will do people good. It is all happiness, submission, kindness and love; it is glory to God in the highest, and good will to man on the earth.—*JD, 14:74*

The doctrine we have heard is good . . . "Secure for yourselves first the kingdom of heaven and its righteousness." When you have done this, every good principle, every good thing, every great endowment, every peaceful influence, and all that can be enjoyed by celestial beings are and will be yours.—*JD, 2:121*

Away with all little meannesses, and deal out kindness to all. From the high and from the lower circles of life find if you can on the face of this earth a gentleman or a lady, in the strict sense of the word, and you will find a man or woman that borders very closely on an angel . . . To be gentle and kind, modest and truthful, to be full of faith and integrity, doing no wrong is of God; goodness sheds a halo of loveliness around every person who possesses it, making their countenances beam with light, and their society desirable because of its excellency. They are loved of God, of holy angels, and of all the good on earth.—*McCloud, 298*

GOSPEL

The laws of the Gospel are neither more nor less than a few of the principles of eternity revealed to the people, by which they can return to heaven from whence they came. We delight in the heavenly law—in that law that will preserve us to all eternity.—*DBY, 1*

We who believe in and have obeyed this Gospel, look forward with the anticipation of obtaining a great amount of knowledge and wisdom. When we embraced the Gospel, the spirit opened up to our minds the fact that the wisdom, the knowledge and the power of God would increase in the midst of the Saints. This is our experience: I, knowing for myself, what the Spirit of the Lord brings to the understanding, testify what it reveals to others.—*JD, 18:236*

The gifts of the Gospel are given to strengthen the faith of the believer.—*DBY, 161*

I wanted to thunder and roar out the Gospel to the nations. It burned in my bones like fire pent up, so I [commenced] to preach the Gospel of life to the people . . . Nothing would satisfy me but to cry abroad in the world, what the Lord was doing in the latter days . . . I had to go out and preach, lest my bones should consume within me.—*McCloud, 33*

Mormonism embraces all truth that is revealed and that is unrevealed, whether religious, political, scientific, or philosophical.—*JD, 9:149*

HAPPINESS

We must know the opposite: know how to contrast, in order to prize and appreciate the comfort and happiness, the joy and the bliss that [we] are actually in possession of . . . Then learn to be happy when you have the privilege.—*JD, 5:294*

To make ourselves happy is incorporated in the great design of man's existence. I have learned not to fret myself about that which I cannot help. If I can do good, I will do it; and if I cannot reach a thing, I will content myself to be without it. This makes me happy all the day long.—*JD, 2:95*

You are greatly blessed of the Lord, all the day long, and should be happy; but we are apt to close our eyes against this fact . . . Were we to look into our own hearts, and seek diligently to do all the good in our power . . . what is there to prevent us from being happy?—*JD, 2:95*

How do you feel, Saints, when you are filled with the power and love of God? You are just as happy as your bodies can bear. What would be your feelings, suppose you should be in prison, and filled with the power and love of God; would you be unhappy? No. I think prisons would palaces prove, if Jesus dwelt there.—*JD, 3:95*

When man is industrious and righteous, then is he happy. Sin blights all true happiness . . . man is always happy when he is righteous.—*JD, 9:244*

There is not that man or woman in this congregation, or on the face of this earth, that has the privilege of the holy Gospel, and lives strictly to it, whom all hell can make unhappy.—*JD, 3:343*

Where is happiness, real happiness? Nowhere but in God. By possessing the spirit of our holy religion, we are happy in the morning, we are happy at noon, we are happy in the evening; for the spirit of love and union is with us, and we rejoice in the spirit because it is of God, and we rejoice in God, for he is the giver of every good thing.—*DBY, 236*

HARDSHIPS

(See Trials and Tribulations)

HEALING

*D*o you suppose that Jesus Christ healed every person that was sick or that all the devils were cast out in the country where he sojourned? I do not. Working miracles, healing the sick, raising the dead, and the like, were almost as rare in his day as in this our day. Once in a while the people would have faith in his power, and what is called a miracle would be performed, but the sick, the blind, the deaf and dumb, the crazy, and those possessed with different kinds of devils were around him, and only now and then could his faith have power to take effect, on account of the want of faith in the individuals.—*JD, 3:45-46*

We lay hands on the sick and wish them to be healed, and pray the Lord to heal them, but we cannot always say that he will.—*JD, 4:284*

When we are prepared, when we are holy vessels before the Lord, a stream of power from the Almighty can pass through the tabernacle of the administrator to the system of the patient, and the sick are made whole; there is virtue in us if we will do right; if we live our religion we are the temples of God wherein he will dwell; if we defile ourselves, these temples God will destroy.—*JD, 14:72*

HEAVEN

I am not going to drive a man or woman to heaven. A great many think that they will be able to flog people into heaven, but this can never be done, for the intelligence in us is as independent as the Gods. People are not to be driven and you can put into a gnat's eye all the souls of the children of men that are driven into heaven by preaching hell-fire.—*DBY, 64*

We have often heard it said . . . that all the heaven we shall ever have is the one we make for ourselves. How vast the meaning of this simple sentence! . . . How is this to be done? By hearkening diligently to the voice of the Spirit of the Lord that entices to righteousness, applauds truth, and exults continually to goodness.—*JD, 9:170*

What a curious doctrine it is, that we are preparing to enjoy! The only heaven for you is that which you make yourselves. My heaven is here—[laying his hand upon his heart]. I carry it with me.—*JD, 4:56*

Do you think the angels of the Lord lust after the things that are before them? All heaven is before us, and all this earth, the gold and the silver, all these are at our command, and shall we lust after them? They are all within our reach; they are for the Saints whom God loves, even all who fix their minds upon Him and the interest of his kingdom.—*JD, 4:44*

HEAVENLY FATHER

(See God)

HELL

*H*as the devil power to afflict, and cast the spirit into torment? No! We have gained ascendency over him. It is in this world only he has power to cause affliction and sickness, pain and distress, sorrow, anguish, and disappointment; but when we go there, behold! The enemy of Jesus has come to the end of his chain; he has finished his work of torment; he cannot come any further; we are beyond his reach.—*JD, 3:95*

We cannot all do as we please, because a great many times we want to and cannot, and that is what produces misery, which is called hell.—*JD, 13:33*

I believe that it is a hell intolerable for a people, a family or a single person, to strive to grasp truth with one hand, and error with the other, to profess to walk in obedience to the commandments of God, and, at the same time, mingle heart and hand with the wicked.—*DBY, 223*

If we will only practice what we profess, I tell you we are at the defiance of hell.—*DBY, 227*

HOLY GHOST

*T*hough a man should say but a few words, and his sentences and words be ever so ungrammatical, if he speaks by the power of the Holy Ghost, he will do good.—*DBY, 31*

Not a desire, act, wish, or thought does the Holy Ghost indulge in contrary to that which is dictated by the Father.—*DBY, 30*

The Holy Ghost is the Spirit of the Lord, and issues forth from himself, and may properly be called God's minister to execute his will in immensity.—*JD, 1:50*

Our faith is concentrated in the Son of God, and through him in the Father; and the Holy Ghost is their minister to bring truths to our remembrance, to reveal new truths to us, and teach, guide, and direct the course of every mind, until we become perfected and prepared to go home, where we can see and converse with our Father in Heaven.—*JD, 6:98*

HONESTY

I have tried to suppress dishonesty in individuals, and have tried thereby to make them honest. If I hire a carpenter and pay him three dollars a day, and he is three days in making a six-panel door that a good workman can make in one, or even a door and a half, I do not want to pay him three dollars a day for that labor.—*JD, 6:73*

Simple truth, simplicity, honesty, uprightness, justice, mercy, love, kindness, do good to all and evil to none, how easy it is to live by such principles! A thousand times easier than to practice deception!—*JD, 14:76*

HUMILITY

The humble will live, their spirits will be buoyant, and they will live to a great age.—*DBY, 228*

The hearts of the meek and humble are full of joy and comfort continually.—*DBY, 228*

It is recorded that Jesus was made perfect through suffering. If he was made perfect through suffering, why should we imagine for one moment that we can be prepared to enter into the kingdom of rest with him and the Father, without passing through similar ordeals?—*JD, 8:66*

We have to humble ourselves and become like little children in our feelings—to become humble and childlike in spirit, in order to receive the first illuminations of the spirit of the Gospel, then we have the privilege of growing, of increasing in knowledge, in wisdom, and in understanding.—*JD, 3:192*

HUSBANDS

*I*t is not my general practice to counsel the sisters to disobey their husbands, but my counsel is—obey your husbands; and I am sanguine and most emphatic on that subject. But I never counselled a woman to follow her husband to the devil. If a man is determined to expose the lives of his friends, let that man go to the devil and to destruction alone.—*JD, 1:77*

Now let me say to the First Presidency, to the Apostles, to all the Bishops in Israel, and to every quorum, and especially to those who are presiding officers, set that example before your wives and your children, before your neighbors and this people, that you can say: "Follow me, as I follow Christ." When we do this, all is right, and our consciences are clear.—*DBY, 198*

Let the husband and father learn to bend his will to the will of his God, and then instruct his wives and children in this lesson of self-government by his example as well as by precept.—*DBY, 198*

IDLENESS: THE IDLER

*I*f you were to divide up our substance now equally amongst this people we would have to do it all over again in a year from now, for the thrifty and careful would have a surplus while the extravagant and shiftless would be without hope and in debt.—*McCloud, 274*

My policy is to keep every man, woman, and child busily employed, that they may have no idle time for hatching mischief in the night, and for making plans to accomplish their own ruin.—*JD, 2:!44*

The Lord's plan is a righteous plan. The wise steward who is willing and industrious should not be made to sacrifice his time and substance to support the idle and shiftless.—*Gates/Widtsoe, 200*

INDUSTRIOUSNESS

*I*f there is impatience in heaven they would be impatient with the slothfulness of the Latter-day Saints. The heavens are waiting to be gracious, and are ready to shed forth all the blessings heaven and earth can bestow on the Saints, as soon as we can receive them and make use of them to the glory of God. If we do not first learn the little things, we cannot learn the greater things.—*JD, 9:296*

Instead of searching after what the Lord is going to do for us, let us inquire what we can do for ourselves.—*JD, 9:172*

To be prudent and saving, and to use the elements in our possession for our benefit and the benefit of our fellow beings is wise and righteous; but to be slothful, wasteful, lazy and indolent, to spend our time and means for naught, is unrighteous.—*JD, 16:16*

When I cannot feed myself through the means God has placed in my power, it is then time enough for Him to exercise His providence in an unusual manner to administer to my wants. But while we can help ourselves, it is our duty to do so . . . While we have a rich soil in this valley, and seed to put in the ground, we need not ask God to feed us, nor follow us around with a loaf of bread begging us to eat it. He will not do it, neither would I, were I the Lord. We can feed ourselves here; and if we are ever placed in circumstances where we cannot, it will be time enough for the Lord to work a miracle to sustain us.—*McCloud, 171*

Let every man and woman be industrious, prudent, and economical in their acts and feelings, and while gathering to themselves, let each one strive to identify his or her interests with the interests of this community, with those of their neighbor and neighborhood, let them seek their happiness and welfare in that of all, and we will be blessed and prospered.—*DBY, 303*

INTELLIGENCE

*E*very branch of knowledge, of wisdom, of light, of understanding, all that I know, all that is within my organization mentally or physically, spiritually or temporally, I have received from some Source.—*JD, 4:266*

The principle is inherent, in the organization of all intelligent beings, so that we are capable of receiving, and receiving and receiving from the inexhaustible fountain of knowledge and truth.—*DBY, 94*

The principle of intelligence is within us. Who planted it there? He who made us. That which you see developed in the children of men . . . is the force of the mind or the spirit, and the body is a tabernacle organized for its temporal habitation.—*JD, 7:286*

The origin of thought and reflection is in ourselves. We think, because we are, and are made susceptible of external influences, and the thoughts of blessing will arise in the same mind, as it is influenced by external circumstances.—*DBY, 52*

Everything in heaven, on earth, and in hell is organized for the benefit, advantage, and exaltation of intelligent beings; therefore there is nothing that is out of the pale of our faith. There is nothing, I may say, good or bad, light or darkness, truth or error, but what is to be controlled by intelligent beings; and we should learn how to take into our possession every blessing and every privilege that God has put within our reach, and know how to use our time, our talents, and all our acts for the advancement of his Kingdom upon the earth.—*JD, 6:145*

No person possesses intelligence, in any degree, that he has not received from the God of heaven, or, in other words, from the Fountain of all intelligence, whether he acknowledges his God in it or not.—*DBY, 148*

JESUS CHRIST

(See Christ)

JOSEPH SMITH

I feel like shouting Hallelujah, all the time, when I think that I ever knew Joseph Smith, the Prophet whom the Lord raised up and ordained, and to whom he gave keys and powers to build up the Kingdom of God on the earth and sustain it.—*JD, 3:51*

From the day that Joseph obtained the plates, and previous to that time, the Lord dictated him. He directed him day by day and hour by hour.—*JD, 8:66*

When you hear a man pour out eternal things, how well you feel, to what a nearness you seem to be brought with God. What a delight it was to hear Brother Joseph talk upon the great principles of eternity; he would bring them down to the capacity of a child, and he would unite heaven with earth, this is the beauty of our religion.—*JD, 4:54*

Now, as bad as myself and my brethren are, and as far as we are from the mark, and from the privileges we should enjoy, if Joseph Smith, Jr., the Prophet, could have seen the people in his day as willing to obey his voice, as they are today to obey the voice of their President, he would have been a happy man. He lived, labored, toiled, and worked; his courage was like the courage of an angel, and his will was like the will of the Almighty, and he labored till they killed him.— *DBY, 464*

Is Joseph glorified? No, he is preaching to the spirits in prison. He will get his resurrection the first of any one in this Kingdom, for he was the first that God made choice of to bring forth the work of the last days.—*DBY, 468*

Those who were acquainted with him [Joseph] knew when the spirit of revelation was upon him, for his countenance wore an expression peculiar to himself while under that influence. He preached by the spirit of revelation, and taught in his council by it, and those who were acquainted with him could discover it at once, for at such times there was a peculiar clearness and transparency in his face.—*Andrus, 35*

I heard the Prophet discourse upon the grandest of subjects. At times he was filled with the Holy Ghost, speaking as with the voice of an archangel and filled with the power of God. His whole person shone, and his face was lightened until it appeared as the whiteness of driven snow.—*Andrus, 34*

Who can say aught against Joseph Smith? I do not think that a man lives on the earth that knew him any better than I did, and I am bold to say that, Jesus Christ excepted, no better man ever lived or does live upon this earth.—*Andrus, 36*

You did not know who you had amongst you. Joseph so loved this people that he gave his life for them; Hyrum loved his brother and this people unto death. Joseph and Hyrum have given their lives for the church. But very few knew Joseph's character; . . . he was in your midst, but you did not know it until after his death . . . Brother Joseph has laid the foundation for a great work, and we will build upon it.—*McCloud, 130*

JOY

*T*he Lord praises you and comforts you if you live as you are directed; if you live with your life hid with Christ in God, you do receive, from the fountain head, life, joy, peace, truth, and every good and wholesome principle that the Lord bestows upon this people, and your hearts exalt in it, and your joy is made full.—*McCloud, 199-200*

...if we lack confidence in each other and become jealous of each other, our peace will be destroyed. If we cultivate the principles of unshaken confidence in each other, our joy will be full.—*McCloud, 183–84*

Strive to be righteous, not for any speculation, but because righteousness is lovely, pure, holy, beautiful, and exalting; it is designed to make the soul happy and full of joy—to the extent of the whole capacity of man, filling him with light, glory, and intelligence.—*JD, 8:172*

JUDGMENT

*I*f you first gain power to check your words, you will then begin to have power to check your judgment, and at length actually gain power to check your thoughts and reflections.—*JD, 6:98*

The Lord's time is not for me to know; but he is kind, long-suffering, and patient, and His wrath endureth silently, and will until mercy is completely exhausted, and then judgment will take the reins. I do not know how, neither do I at present wish to know. It is enough for us to know how to serve our God and live our religion, and thus we will increase in the favor of God.—*JD, 4:371*

Let us be patient one with another. I do not altogether look at things as you do. My judgment is not in all things like yours, nor yours like mine. When you judge a man or woman, judge the intentions of the heart. It is not by words, particularly, nor by actions, that men will be judged in the great day of the Lord; but, in connection with words and actions, the sentiments and intentions of the heart will be taken, and by these will men be judged.—*JD, 8:10*

I do know that the trying day will soon come to you and to me; and ere long we will have to lay down these tabernacles and go into the spirit world. And I do know that as we lie down, so judgment will find us, and that is scriptural; "as the tree falls so it shall lie," or, in other words, as death leaves us so judgment will find us.—*JD, 4:52*

KINGDOM OF GOD

When the Kingdom is organized in any age, the Spirit of it dwells in the hearts of the faithful, while its visible department exists among the people, with laws, ordinances, helps, governments, officers, administrators, and every appendage necessary for its complete operation to the attainment of the end in view.—*DBY, 441*

No man will gain influence in this Kingdom, save what he gains by the influence and power of the Holy One that has called him to truth, holiness, and virtue. That is all the influence I have, and I pray God that I may never have any different influence.—*McCloud, 156*

We must watch and pray, and look well to our walk and conversation, and live near to our God, that the love of this world may not choke the precious seed of truth, and feel ready, if necessary, to offer up all things, even life itself, for the Kingdom of Heaven's sake.—*JD, 11:111*

God has commenced to set up his kingdom on the earth, and all hell and its devils are moving against it. Hell is yawning and sending forth its devils and their imps. What for? To destroy the kingdom of God from the earth. But they cannot do it.—*JD, 5:74,75*

The Kingdom we are talking about, preaching about and trying to build up is the Kingdom of God on the earth, not in the starry heavens, nor in the sun. We are trying to establish the Kingdom of God on the earth to which really and properly everything that pertains to men—their feelings, their faith, their affections, their desires, and every act of their lives—belong, that they may be ruled by it spiritually and temporally.—*JD, 10:328*

KNOWLEDGE

When we get to understand all knowledge, all wisdom, that it is necessary for us to understand in the flesh, we will be like clay in the hands of the potter, willing to be moulded and fashioned according to the will of him who has called us to this great and glorious work, of purifying ourselves and our fellow-beings, and of preparing the nations of the earth for the glory that awaits them through obedience.—*DBY, 223*

I shall not cease learning while I live, nor when I arrive in the spirit-world; but shall there learn with greater facility; and when I again receive my body, I shall learn a thousand times more in a thousand times less time, and then I do not mean to cease learning but shall still continue my researches.—*Gates/Widtsoe, 283*

Let there be a mutual desire in every man to disseminate knowledge, that all may know.—*JD, 9:370*

When we speak of education, it is not to be understood that it alone consists in a man's learning the letters of the alphabet, in being trained in every branch of scholastic lore, in becoming proficient in the knowledge of the sciences, and a classical scholar—but also in learning to classify himself and others...We are in a great school, and we should be diligent to learn...and read good books ...and extract from them wisdom and understanding as much as you possibly can, aided by the Spirit of God.—*Gates/Widtsoe, 281*

Education is the hand-maid to honest labor.—*JD, 9:370*

LABOR

*T*hey who secure eternal life are doers of the word as well as hearers.—*JD, 14:37*

Do those things that are necessary to be done and let those alone that are not necessary, and we shall accomplish more than we do now.—*JD, 3:160*

Everything connected with building up Zion requires actual, severe labor. It is nonsense to talk about building up any kingdom except by labor; it requires the labor of every part of our organization, whether it be mental, physical, or spiritual, and that is the only way to build up the Kingdom of God.—*DBY, 291*

Whatever the Latter-day Saints have gained has been obtained by sheer wrestling and unconquerable resolution.—*JD, 13:93*

Time and the ability to labor are the capital stock of the whole world of mankind, and we are all indebted to God for the ability to use time to advantage.—*DBY, 301*

Follow the spirit of improvement and labor. All the capital there is upon the earth is the bone and sinew of working men and women.—JD, 16:66

Let the Latter-day Saints neglect their labor, and they will soon find that they are declining in their feelings, tastes and judgments for improving the elements of the earth.—JD, 16:66

LAST DAYS

*J*oseph Smith has laid the foundation of the Kingdom of God in the last days; others will rear the superstructure.—*JD, 9:364*

All that Joseph Smith did was to preach the truth—the Gospel as the Lord revealed it to him—and tell the people how to be saved, and the honest-in-heart ran together and gathered around him and loved him as they did their own lives. He could do no more than to preach true principles, and that will gather the Saints in the last days, even the honest-in-heart. All who believe and obey the Gospel of Jesus Christ are his witnesses to the truth of these statements.—*JD, 10:326*

The Lord has done his share of the work; he has surrounded us with elements containing wheat, meat, flax, wool, silk, fruit, and everything with which to build up, beautify and glorify the Zion of the last days, and it is our business to mould these elements to our wants and necessities, according to the knowledge we now have and the wisdom we can obtain from the heavens through our faithfulness. In this way will the Lord bring again Zion upon the earth, and in no other.—*JD, 9:283*

LIBERTY

*L*ife and death are set before us, and we are at liberty to choose which we will... to choose life is to choose an eternal existence in an organized capacity: to refuse life and choose death is to refuse an eternal existence in an organized capacity, and be contented to become decomposed, and return again to native element.—*JD, 1:340*

There is not a man of us but what is willing to acknowledge at once that God demands strict obedience to his requirements. But in rendering that strict obedience, are we made slaves? No, it is the only way on the face of the earth for you and me to become free.—*DBY, 225*

God rules and reigns, and has made all his children as free as himself, to choose the right or the wrong, and we shall then be judged according to our works.—*DBY, 55*

LIFE

*H*uman beings are expected by their Creator to be actively employed in doing good every day of their lives, either in improving their own mental and physical condition, or that of their neighbors.—*DBY, 88*

This life is now the only life to us; and if we do not appreciate it properly it is impossible to prepare for a higher and more exalted life.—*JD, 10:222*

The object of this existence is to learn, which we can only do a little at a time.—*DBY, 87*

This people must go forward, or they will go backward.—*JD, 16:165*

Instead of preparing to die, prepare to live in the midst of all the exaltations of the Gods.—*JD, 9:291*

This is a world in which we are to prove ourselves. The lifetime of man is a day of trial, wherein we may prove to God—in our darkness, in our weakness, and where the enemy reigns—that we are our Father's friends.—*McCloud, 299*

It is our privilege to say, every day of our lives, "That is the best day I ever lived." Never let a day so pass that you will have cause to say, "I will live better tomorrow," and I will promise you, in the name of the Lord Jesus Christ, that your lives will be as a well of water springing up to everlasting life. You will have his Spirit to dwell in you continually, and your eyes will be open to see, your ears to hear, and your understanding to comprehend.—*DBY, 90*

LIGHT

*T*he Spirit of the Lord enlightens every man that comes into the world. There is no one that lives upon the earth but what is, more or less, enlightened by the Spirit of the Lord Jesus. It is said of him, that He is the light of the world. He lighteth every man that comes into the world and every person, at times, has the light of the spirit of truth upon him.—*DBY, 32*

For a man to undertake to live a Saint and walk in darkness is one of the hardest tasks that he can undertake. You cannot imagine a position that will sink a person more deeply in perplexity and trouble than to try to be a Saint without living as a Saint should—without enjoying the spirit of his religion. It is our privilege to live so as to enjoy the spirit of our religion. That is designed to restore us to the presence of the Gods. Gods exist, and we had better strive to be prepared to be one with them.—*DBY, 227*

In every man there is a candle of the Lord which burns with a clear light; and if by the wickedness of a man it is extinguished, then farewell for ever to that individual.—*JD, 9:104*

LOVE

Neither will you or I believe that anybody loves us and wishes to promote our joy and comfort, so long as that person acts contrary thereto; neither will Jesus. And unless these Latter-day Saints stop now, and go to work and prove by their acts that they are the disciples of the Lord Jesus, He will spew them out.—*JD, 17:40,41*

It should be satisfactory evidence that you are in the path of life, if you love God and your brethren with all your hearts.—*DBY, 271*

It is folly in the extreme for persons to say that they love God; when they do not love their brethren.—*DBY, 271*

Be just as independent as a God to do good. Love mercy, eschew evil, be a savior to yourselves and to your families.—*JD, 15:7*

Men should act upon the principle of righteousness, because it is right, and is a principle which they love to cherish and see practiced by all men. They should love mercy, because of its benevolence, charity, love, clemency, and all of its lovely attributes, and be inspired thereby to deal justly, fairly, honorably, meting out to others their just deservings.—*JD, 1:119*

God bless the humble and the righteous, and may He have compassion upon us because of the weakness that is in our nature. And considering the great weakness and ignorance of mortals, let us have mercy upon each other.—*McCloud, 299*

MAN

*G*od has made His children like Himself to stand erect, and has endowed them with intelligence and power and dominion over all His works, and given them the same attributes which He Himself possesses.—*JD, 11:122*

Who can define the divinity of man? Man, by being exalted, does not lose the power and ability naturally given to him; but, on the contrary, by taking the road that leads to life, he gains more power, more influence and ability every step he progresses therein.—*JD, 7:274*

We were created upright, pure and holy, in the image of our father and our mother, the image of our God.—*JD, 3:365*

The greatest lesson you can learn is to learn yourselves . . . you cannot learn it immediately, neither can all the philosophy of the age teach it to you: you have to come here to get a practical experience and to learn yourselves. You will then begin to learn more perfectly the things of God. No being can thoroughly learn himself, without understanding more or less of the things of God: neither can any being learn and understand the things of God, without learning himself.—*JD, 8:334-35*

The Lord will bring about the results, and mankind cannot prevent it. The wicked may design an evil against the righteous, and he causes it to result in good. That is making the wrath of man praise him. He has not granted to man to bring out the result of his works . . . that power he retains to himself.—*JD, 8:31*

MARRIAGE

I tell you here, now, in the presence of the Almighty God, it is not the privilege of any Elder to have even one wife, before he has honored his Priesthood, before he has magnified his calling. If you obtain one, it is by mere permission, to see what you will do, how you will act, whether you will conduct yourself in righteousness in that holy estate. Take care! Elders of Israel, be cautious! Or you will lose your wives and your children.—*JD, 1:119*

The Lord says—Let my servants and handmaidens be sealed, and let their children be sealed.—*DBY, 195*

Be careful, O ye mothers in Israel, and do not teach your daughters in future, as many of them have been taught, to marry out of Israel. Woe to you who do it; you will lose your crowns as sure as God lives.—*DBY, 196*

But the whole subject of the marriage relation is not in my reach, nor in any other man's reach on this earth. It is without beginning of days or end of years; it is a hard matter to reach. We can tell some things with regard to it; it lays the foundation for worlds, for angels, and for the Gods; for intelligent beings to be crowned with glory, immortality, and eternal lives. In fact, it is the thread which runs from the beginning to the end of the holy Gospel of Salvation—of the Gospel of the Son of God; it is from eternity to eternity.—*JD, 2:90*

MEETINGS

*I*f there is a Bishop's meeting, let every Bishop, Priest, Teacher and Deacon attend, and no man among them say, "I must go and water my grain," "cut my hay," or "gather my harvest;" but attend the meeting, sit until it is out and hear every word. If you have to speak, speak; if you are to hear only, hear every word that is said.—*JD, 15:35*

There are a great many people in this city who should attend meeting on a Sunday morning— enough to fill this house, besides those who go to Sunday school...but they are here, there and everywhere but where they should be...will you ...set the example, and come to meetings every Sunday? Or shall I, in a few Sundays, hear that you are gone on a pleasure excursion, that you are riding out here or there?—*JD, 14:221*

I shall require the people to be perfectly still, while they are here and we are trying to speak to them. Let there be no talking, whispering, nor shuffling of feet. It would be beneficial for mothers who have small children here that will cry, to leave the bowery, if they cannot keep their children still.—*JD, 4:112*

On one occasion when he [Brigham] learned that one of his children was very ill and calling for him he stopped a council meeting declaring to the assembly that the meeting could wait, but his sick child could not.—*Gates/Widtsoe, 340*

MELCHIZEDEK PRIESTHOOD

I have tried to show you, brethren, as briefly as possible, the order of the Priesthood. When a man is ordained to be an Apostle, his Priesthood is without beginning of days, or end of life, like the Priesthood of Melchizedek; for it was his Priesthood that was spoken of in this language and not the man.—*JD, 1:136*

I do not care who leads this Church, even though it were Ann Lee; but one thing I must know, and that is what God says about it. I have the keys and the means of obtaining the mind of God on the subject . . . Joseph conferred upon our heads all the keys and powers belonging to the Apostleship which he himself held before he was taken away, and no man or set of men can get between Joseph and the Twelve.—*McCloud, 127*

MESSIAH

(See Christ)

MIRACLES

The providences of God are all a miracle to the human family until they understand them. There are no miracles only to those who are ignorant. A miracle is supposed to be a result without a cause, but there is no such thing.—*JD, 14:79*

Miracles, or those extraordinary manifestations of the power of God, are not for the unbeliever; they are to console the Saints, and to strengthen and confirm the faith of those who love, fear, and serve God.—*JD, 12:97*

In the Christian world it is generally conceded that signs are no longer necessary, and that miracles are not needed now . . . I do not so understand it . . . I believe that miracles are as absolutely necessary now as they ever were . . . these miracles or manifestations of the power of God, though not believed in by the Christian world, are necessary for you and me and for all who wish to be blessed by their means . . . After obedience to these requirements (the Gospel) an individual is entitled to and may enjoy the blessing of miracles just as well as Jesus did.—JD, 13:140, 41

So when individuals are blessed with visions, revelations, and great manifestations, look out, then the Devil is nigh you, and you will be tempted in proportion to the visions, revelation, or manifestation you have received.—DBY, 338

MISSIONARIES/
MISSIONARY WORK

I would like to impress upon the minds of the brethren, that he who goes forth in the name of the Lord, trusting in Him with all his heart, will never want for wisdom to answer any question that is asked him, or to give any counsel that may be required to lead the people in the way of life and salvation, and he will never be confounded, worlds without end. Go in the name of the Lord, trust in the name of the Lord, lean upon the Lord, and call upon the Lord fervently and without ceasing, and pay no attention to the world.—*JD, 12:34*

The Gospel must be preached to the world, that the wicked may be left without excuse.—*DBY, 317*

We had better gather nine that are unworthy than to neglect the tenth if he is worthy.—*DBY, 321*

Our Father in Heaven, Jesus, our Elder Brother and the Savior of the world, and the whole heavens, are calling upon this people to prepare to save the nations of the earth, also the millions who have slept without the Gospel.—*DBY, 317*

If to all eternity you could praise God, through the means of saving one soul, I may say the least or most inferior intelligence upon the earth, pertaining to the human family—if you could be the means of saving one such person, how great would be your joy in the heavens! Then let us save many, and our joy will be great in proportion to the number of souls we save. Let us destroy none.—*JD, 9:124*

Ever strive to be humble, faithful and obedient, calling upon the Lord in faith and sincerity, and he will fill you with wisdom and understanding, give you power to influence the honest in heart, guide, bless and protect you, and crown your faithful labors with a success that it has not entered into your heart to conceive possible.—*Jessee, 28*

MORMONISM

I will tell you in a few words what I understand "Mormonism" to be . . . it embraces every fact there is in the heavens and in the heaven of heavens—every fact there is upon the surface of the earth, in the bowels of the earth, and in the starry heavens; in fine, it embraces all truth there is in all the eternities of the Gods. How, then, can we deny it?—*McCloud, 24*

I did not embrace Mormonism because I hoped it was true, but because I knew it was that principle that would save all the human family that would obey it.—*McCloud, 109*

"Mormonism" keeps men and women young and handsome; and when they are full of the Spirit of God, there are none of them but what will have a glow upon their countenances; and that is what makes you and me young; for the Spirit of God is with us and within us.—*JD, 5:210*

The design of the Gospel is to reveal the secrets of the hearts of the children of men.—*DBY, 446*

All knowledge and wisdom and every good that the heart of man can desire is within the circuit and circle of the faith we have embraced.—*JD, 13:150*

When people receive this Gospel, what do they sacrifice? Why, death for life. This is what they give: darkness for light, error for truth, doubt and unbelief for knowledge and the certainty of the things of God.—*JD, 16:161*

MORTALITY

(See Life)

MOTHERS

A child loves the smiles of its mother, but hates her frowns. I tell the mothers not to allow the children to indulge in evils, but at the same time to treat them with mildness. If a child is required to step in a certain direction, and it does not seem willing to do so, gently put it in the desired way, and say, "There, my little dear, you must step when I speak to you." Children need directing and teaching what is right in a kind, affectionate manner.—*JD, 8:74*

The first thing that is taught by the mother to the child should be true; we should never allow ourselves to teach our children one thing and practice another.—*DBY, 206*

If a mother wishes to control her child, in the first place let her learn to control herself, that she may be successful in bringing the child into perfect submission to her will.—*JD, 14:277*

I wish the daughters of Israel to far exceed their mothers in wisdom.—*DBY, 205*

It is the calling of the wife and mother to know what to do with everything that is brought into the house, labouring to make her home desirable to her husband and children, making herself an Eve in the midst of a little paradise of her own creating, securing her husband's love and confidence, and tying her offspring to herself, with a love that is stronger than death, for an everlasting inheritance.—*McCloud, 287*

MUSIC

*I*t has been proved that sweet music will actually tame the most malicious and venomous beasts . . . and make them docile and harmless as lambs. Who gave the lower animals a love for those sweet sounds, which with magic power fill the air with harmony, and cheer and comfort the hearts of men, and so wonderfully affect the brute creation? It was the Lord, our heavenly Father, who gave the capacity to enjoy these sounds, and which we ought to do in His name, and to His glory.—*JD, 1:48*

I want it distinctly understood, that fiddling and dancing are no part of our worship. The question may be asked, What are they for, then? I answer, that my body may keep pace with my mind . . . they give me a privilege to throw everything off, and shake myself, that my body may exercise, and my mind rest.—*McCloud, 166*

Music belongs to heaven, to cheer God, angels and men . . . Music and dancing are for the benefit of holy ones, and all those who are not holy and righteous and who do not worship God, have no right to be here.—*McCloud, 196*

MYSTERIES

hat is a mystery? We do not know, it is beyond our comprehension. When we talk about mystery, we talk about eternal obscurity; for that which is known, ceases to be a mystery; and all that is known, we may know as we progress in the scale of intelligence.—*JD, 1:274*

These are the mysteries of the Kingdom of God upon the earth, to know how to purify and sanctify our affections, the earth upon which we stand, the air we breathe, the water we drink, the houses in which we dwell and the cities we build, that when strangers come into our country they may feel a hallowed influence and acknowledge a power to which they are strangers.—*DBY, 339*

You may now be inclined to say, "We wish to hear the mysteries of the kingdoms of the Gods who have existed from eternity, and of all the kingdoms in which they will dwell; we desire to have these things portrayed to our understanding." Allow me to inform you that you are in the midst of it all now, that you are in just as good a kingdom as you will ever attain to, from now to all eternity, unless you make it yourselves by the grace of God, by the will of God, which is a code of laws perfectly calculated to govern and control eternal matter.—*DBY, 339*

OBEDIENCE

*T*he expression, "true believer," needs qualifying, for many believe who do not obey—I will qualify it by saying, a believer in Jesus Christ, who manifests his faith to God, angels, and his brethren, by his obedience. Not but that there are believers who do not obey, but the only true believers are they who prove their belief by their obedience to the requirements of the Gospel.—*JD, 1:234*

I am responsible for the doctrine I teach; but I am not responsible for the obedience of the people to that doctrine.—*JD, 13:1*

A mere theory amounts to but little, while practice and obedience have to do with stern realities.—*JD, 9:330*

We should never permit ourselves to do anything that we are not willing to see our children do. We should set them an example that we wish them to imitate. Do we realize this? How often we see parents demand obedience, good behavior, kind words, pleasant looks, a sweet voice and a bright eye from a child or children when they themselves are full of bitterness and scolding! How inconsistent and unreasonable this is!—JD, 14:192

ONENESS

(See Unity)

PARENTS

hen children are old enough to labor in the field, then the father will take them in charge. If children are not taught by their mothers, in the days of their youth, to revere and follow the counsels of their fathers, it will be hard indeed for the father ever to control them.—*JD, 1:68*

Teach your children from their youth, never to set their hearts immoderately upon an object of this world.—*JD, 3:357*

If the law of Christ becomes the tradition of this people, the children will be brought up according to the law of the celestial kingdom, else they are not brought up in the way they should go.—*DBY, 207*

Parents, have you ever noticed that your children have exercised faith for you when you have been sick? The little daughter, seeing you sick, will lift her heart with a pure, angelic-like prayer to heaven; and disease is rebuked when that kind of faith is exercised. God bless the children! I pray that they may live and be reared up in righteousness, that God may have a people that will spread and establish one universal reign of peace, and possess the powers of the world to come.—*JD, 8:117*

PEACE

*L*et us so live that the spirit of our religion will live within us, then we have peace, joy, happiness and contentment, which makes for pleasant fathers, pleasant mothers, pleasant children, pleasant house-holds, neighbors, communities and cities. That is worth living for, and I do think that the Latter-day Saints ought to strive for this.—*JD, 15:135*

Mankind has forfeited the right they once possessed to the friendship of their Heavenly Father, and through sin have exposed themselves to misery and wretchedness. Who is to bring back to the sin-stained millions of earth that which they have lost through disobedience? Who is to plant smiling peace and plenty where war and desolation reign? Who is to remove the curse and its consequences from earth—the homestead of mankind? Who shall say to the raging and contending elements, "Peace, be still," and extract the poison from the reptile's tooth, and the savage and destructive nature from beast and creeping thing? . . . All this will be accomplished through the law of the holy Priesthood.—*DBY, 99*

Great peace have they who love the law of the Lord and abide in his commandments.—JD, *8:121*

PERFECTION

*D*o not suppose that we shall ever in the flesh be free from temptations to sin. Some suppose that they can in the flesh be sanctified body and spirit and become so pure that they will never again feel the effects of the power of the adversary of truth. Were it possible for a person to attain to this degree of perfection in the flesh, he could not die neither remain in a world where sin predominates . . . All the Lord has called us to do is to renovate our own hearts . . .—*JD, 10:173*

Though we are in the world, yet we should be as perfect as mortals are required to be. We are not required in our sphere to be as perfect as Gods and angels are in their spheres, yet man is the king of kings and lord of lords in embryo.—*JD, 10:223*

To be as perfect as we possibly can, according to our knowledge, is to be just as perfect as our Father in heaven is. He cannot be any more perfect than He knows how, any more than we. When we are doing as well as we know how in the sphere and station which we occupy here, we are justified in the justice, righteousness, mercy, and judgment that go before the Lord of heaven and earth. We are as justified as the angels who are before the throne of God. The sin that will cleave to all the posterity of Adam and Eve is, that they have not done as well as they knew how.—*JD, 2:129-30*

PERSEVERANCE

By order and perseverance combined with a reliance on the Lord you are bound to progress . . . and make a useful man in the midst of God's people.—*Jessee, 223*

Never allow your courage to fail you; man's greatest works have been done by men of patience, perseverance, and a determined will which would acknowledge no defeat.—*Jessee, 249*

Nothing worthy of obtaining is ever engaged by us without perseverance. "There is no excellency without labor." You must, therefore, strive on.— *Jessee, 313*

The men and women who desire to obtain seats in the celestial kingdom, will find that they must battle with the enemy of all righteousness every day . . . "take the helmet of salvation, and the sword of the Spirit, which is the word of God; praying always with all prayer and supplication in the spirit, and watching there unto with all perseverance and supplication . . . " Let us see to it that we are ready for the enemy, to baffle him at every point, contending bravely against him until he is successfully repulsed.—*JD, 11:14,15*

PLEASURES

(See Worldliness)

PRAYER

*L*et every man and every woman call upon the name of the Lord, and that, too, from a pure heart, while they are at work as well as in their closet; while they are in public as well as while they are in private, asking the Father in the name of Jesus, to bless them, and to preserve and guide in, and to teach them, the way of life and salvation and to enable them so to live that they will obtain this eternal salvation we are after.—*JD, 15:63*

Practice your religion today, and say your prayers faithfully.—*DBY, 42*

I shall not ask the Lord to do what I am not willing to do.—*DBY, 43*

Your prayers cannot prevail if there is disunion among you.—*JD, 7:274*

If the Devil says you cannot pray when you are angry, tell him it is none of his business, and pray until that species of insanity is dispelled and serenity is restored to the mind.—*JD, 10:175*

It matters not whether you or I feel like praying, when the time comes to pray, pray . . . You will find that those who wait til the Spirit bids them pray, will never pray much on this earth.—*JD, 13:155*

To daughter, Susa, when she asked how she could know the Gospel was true: "Daughter, there is only one way to find it out. And that is the way I found it out and the way your mother found it out. Get down on your knees and ask God to give you that testimony and knowledge which

Peter had when Christ asked the Apostles, 'whom do ye say that I am?'"—*Gates/Widtsoe, 9*

If we draw near to him, he will draw near to us; if we seek him early, we shall find him; if we apply our minds faithfully and diligently day by day, to know and understand the mind and will of God, it is as easy, yes, I will say easier than it is to know the minds of each other, for to know and understand ourselves and our own being is to know and understand God and his being.—*JD, 13:312*

PRIESTHOOD

*I*f anybody wants to know what the Priesthood of the Son of God is, it is the law by which the worlds are, were, and will continue for ever and ever. It is that system which brings worlds into existence and peoples them, gives them revolutions—their days, weeks, months, years, their seasons and times by which they are rolled up as a scroll, as it were, and go into a higher state of existence.—*JD, 15:127*

The Priesthood does not wait for ignorance; it instructs those who have not wisdom, and are desirous of learning correct principles.—*JD, 7:64*

An individual who holds a share in the Priesthood, and continues faithful to his calling, who delights himself continually in doing the things God requires at his hands, and continues through life in the performance of every duty will secure to himself not only the privilege of receiving, but the knowledge how to receive the things of God, that he may know the mind of God continually; and he will be enabled to discern between right and wrong, between the things of God and the things that are not of God. And the Priesthood—the Spirit that is within him, will continue to increase until it becomes like a fountain of living water; until it is like the tree of life; until it is one continued source of intelligence and instruction to that individual.—*JD, 3:192*

Until a selfish, individual interest is banished from our minds, and we become interested in the general welfare, we shall never be able to magnify our holy Priesthood as we should.—*DBY, 133*

There is no law to prevent any man from obtaining all the blessings of the priesthood if he will walk according to the commandments, pay his tithes and seek after salvation, but he may deprive himself of them . . .—*McCloud, 136*

All ye inhabitants of the earth, hearken and hear! God has, in our day, spoken from the heavens; he has bestowed his holy Priesthood on the children of men; he has called upon people to repent. Let us submit to him, that we may share in this invisible, almighty, God-like power, which is the everlasting Priesthood.—*JD, 3:259*

PROPHECY

The inquiry may be made, "Can any person in the world prophesy, unless he possess the spirit of it?" No, they cannot. They may prophesy lies by the spirit of lies, by the inspiration of a lying spirit, but can they see and understand things in the future, so as to prophesy truly of things to come, unless they are endowed with the spirit of prophecy? No.—*JD, 3:89*

Does the gift of prophecy exist with us? This fact is so evident and plain that it appears to us almost a loss of time to talk about it. The present state of our once happy country, I have preached and prophesied of for the last thirty years; and so have thousands of others prophesied before the people of this land that the Almighty would come out in his wrath and vex the nation for persecuting the Priesthood of the Son of God: the fulfilment is too evident to attempt to prove.—*JD, 10:324*

RECREATION

(See Dance)

REDEMPTION

(See Atonement)

RELIEF SOCIETY

I will here say to the Latter-day Saints, if you will feed the poor with a willing heart and ready hand, neither you nor your children will ever be found begging bread. In these things the people are right; they are right in establishing Female Relief Societies, that the hearts of the widow and the orphan may be made glad by the blessings which are so abundantly and so freely poured out upon them.—*JD, 12:171*

As I have often told my sisters in the Female Relief Societies, we have sisters here who, if they had the privilege of studying, would make just as good mathematicians or accountants as any man; and we think they ought to have the privilege to study these branches of knowledge that they may develop the powers with which they are endowed. We believe that women are useful, not only to sweep houses, wash dishes, make beds, and raise babies, but that they should stand behind the counter, study law or physics, or become good bookkeepers and be able to do the business in any counting house, and all this to enlarge their sphere of usefulness for the benefit of society at large. In following these things they but answer the design of their creation.—*JD, 13:61*

The sisters in our Female Relief Societies have done great good. Can you tell the amount of good that the mothers and daughters in Israel are capable of doing? No, it is impossible. And the good they will do will follow them to all eternity.—*JD, 13:34*

REPENTANCE

*W*hen men truly and heartily repent, and make manifest to the heavens that their repentance is genuine by obedience to the requirements made known to them through the laws of the Gospel, they are entitled to the administration of salvation, and no power can withhold the good spirit from them.—*JD, 10:18*

Though we may do the best we know how at this time, can there be no improvement made in our lives? There can. If we do wrong ignorantly, when we learn it is wrong, then it is our duty to refrain from that wrong immediately and for ever, and the sin of ignorance is winked at, and passes into oblivion.—*JD, 2:130*

Sin consists in doing wrong when we know and can do better, and it will be punished with a just retribution, in the due time of the Lord.—*JD, 2:133*

Keep your follies that do not concern others to yourselves, and keep your private wickedness as still as possible; hide it from the eyes of the public gaze as far as you can. I wish to say this upon this particular point in regard to people's confessing. We wish to see people honestly confess as they should and what they should.—*JD, 8:361*

The Savior has warned us to be careful how we judge, forgiving each other seven times seventy in a day, if we repent, and confess our sins one to another. Can we be more merciful and forgiving than our Father in Heaven? We cannot. Therefore let people do the best they can, and they will pave the way for the rising generation to walk up into the light, wisdom, and knowledge of the angels, and of the redeemed from this earth, to say nothing of other earths, and they will be prepared to enjoy in the resurrection all the blessings which are for the faithful, and enjoy them in the flesh.—*DBY, 157*

RESURRECTION

After the spirit leaves the body, it remains without a tabernacle in the spirit world until the Lord, by his law that he has ordained, brings to pass the resurrection of the dead. When the angel who holds the keys of the resurrection shall sound his trumpet, then the peculiar fundamental principles that organized our bodies here, if we do honor to them, though they be deposited in the depths of the sea, and though one particle is in the north, another in the south, another in the east, and another in the west, will be brought together again in the twinkling of an eye, and our spirits will take possession of them. We shall then be prepared to dwell with the Father and the Son, and we never can be prepared to dwell with them until then. Spirits, when they leave their bodies, do not dwell with the Father and the Son, but live in the Spirit world, where there are places prepared for them.

Those who do honor to their tabernacles, and love and believe in the Lord Jesus Christ, must put off this mortality, or they cannot put on immortality. This body must be changed, else it cannot be prepared to dwell in the glory of the Father.—*JD, 8:28*

Now understand, to choose life is to choose principles that will lead you to an eternal increase, and nothing short of them will produce life in the resurrection for the faithful. Those that choose death, make choice of the path which leads to the end of their organization. The one leads to endless increase and progression, the other to the destruction.—*JD, 1:352*

The earth will abide its creation, and will be counted worthy of receiving the blessings designed for it, and will ultimately roll back into the presence of God who formed it and established its mineral, vegetable, and animal kingdoms. These will all be retained upon the earth, come forth in the resurrection, and abide for ever and for ever.—*JD, 8:8*

I wish men would look upon that eternity which is before them. In the great morning of the resurrection, with what grief would they look upon their little trifling affairs of this probation; they would say, "O! Do not mention it, for it is a source of mortification to me to think that I ever should be guilty of doing wrong, or of neglecting to do good to my fellow men, even if they have abused me."—*JD, 1:32*

REVELATION

*N*o earthly argument, no earthly reasoning can open the minds of intelligent beings and show them heavenly things; that can only be done by the Spirit of revelation.—*DBY, 37*

How can you know the Latter-day work to be true? You can know it only by the spirit of revelation direct from Heaven.—*DBY, 36*

But we should all live so that the Spirit of revelation could dictate and write on the heart and tell us what we should do instead of the traditions of our parents and teachers. But to do this we must become like little children; and Jesus says if we do not we cannot enter the kingdom of heaven. How simple it is! Live free from envy, malice, wrath, strife, bitter feelings, and evil speaking in our families and about our neighbors and friends and all the inhabitants of the earth, wherever we meet them. Live so that our consciences are free, clean and clear.—*JD, 14:161*

No man can know Jesus the Christ except it be revealed from heaven to him.—*DBY, 37*

There are revelations, wisdom, knowledge, and understanding yet to be proclaimed.—*DBY, 39*

There is not a man upon the earth who can magnify even an earthly office, without the power and wisdom of God to aid him.—*DBY, 34*

Without the light of the Spirit of Christ, no person can truly enjoy life.—*DBY, 34*

When a revelation is given to any people, they must walk according to it, or suffer the penalty which is the punishment of disobedience, but when the word is, "will you do thus and so?" "It is the mind and will of God that you perform such and such a duty," the consequences of disobedience are not so dreadful, as they would be if the word of the Lord were to be written under the declaration, "Thus saith the Lord."—*JD, 12:127*

RIGHTEOUSNESS

Strive to be righteous, not for any speculation, but because righteousness is lovely, pure, holy, beautiful, and exalting: it is designed to make the soul happy and full of joy, to the extent of the whole capacity of man, filling him with light, glory, and intelligence.—*JD, 8:172*

No blessing that is sealed upon us will do us any good, unless we live for it.—*JD, 11:117*

God has promised you, Jesus has promised you, and the Apostles and Prophets of old and of our day have promised you that you shall be rewarded according to all you can desire in righteousness before the Lord, if you live for that reward.—*JD, 8: 197*

When we speak, let us speak good words; when we think, let us think good thoughts; and when we act, perform good acts; until it shall become the delight of every man and woman to do good instead of evil, and to teach righteousness by example and precept.—*JD, 10:360*

I say again—"Seek ye first the kingdom of God and His righteousness," and in due time, no matter when, "all these things" (that appear so necessary to have in the world) "shall be added unto you." Everything that is in heaven, on the earth, and in the earth, everything the most fruitful mind can imagine, shall be yours.—*JD, 2:125*

Righteousness in whomsoever found, will never lead you astray.—*JD, 2:125*

SABBATH

*N*ow, remember, my brethren, those who go skating, buggy riding or on excursions on the Sabbath day—and there is a great deal of this practiced—are weak in the faith. Gradually, little by little, the spirit of their religion leaks out of their hearts and their affections, and by and by they begin to see faults in their brethren, faults in the doctrines of the Church, faults in the organization, and at last they leave the Kingdom of God and go to destruction. I really wish you would remember this, and tell it to your neighbors.—*JD, 15:83*

I said yesterday to a Bishop who was mending a breach in the canal, and expressed a wish to continue his labor on the following Sabbath, as his wheat was burning up, let it burn, when the time comes that is set apart for worship, go up and worship the Lord.—*JD, 3:331*

The Lord has directed his people to rest one-seventh part of the time, and we take the first day of the week, and call it our Sabbath. This is according to the order of the Christians. We should observe this for our own temporal good and spiritual welfare . . . six days are enough for us to work, and if we wish to play, play within the six days; if we wish to go on excursions, take one of those six days, but on the seventh day, come to the place of worship, attend to the Sacrament, confess your faults one to another and to our God, and pay attention to the ordinances of the house of God.—*JD, 15:81*

SACRAMENT

*T*he revelations of God to Joseph Smith instruct the Latter-day Saints to live their religion day by day, and to meet on the first day of the week to break bread, confess their faults one to another, and pray with and for each other. I would like this tradition fastened not only upon the people generally, but particularly upon the Bishops and other leaders of this Church.—*JD, 9:369*

I say to the brethren and sisters, in the name of the Lord, it is our duty and it is required of us, by our Father in Heaven, by the spirit of our religion, by our covenants with God and each other, that we observe the ordinances of the house of God, and especially on the Sabbath day, to attend to the Sacrament of the Lord's Supper. Then attend the Ward meetings and the Quorum meetings.—*JD, 15:82*

SALVATION

*S*alvation is the full existence of man, of the angels, and the Gods; it is eternal life—the life which was, which is, and which is to come. And we, as human beings, are heirs to all this life, if we apply ourselves strictly to obey the requirements of the law of God, and continue in faithfulness.—*JD, 12:111*

How do we know that prophets wrote the word of the Lord? By revelation . . . Without revelation direct from heaven, it is impossible for any person to understand fully the plan of salvation . . . I say that the living oracles of God, or the Spirit of revelation must be in each and every individual, to know the plan of salvation and keep in the path that leads them to the presence of God.— *McCloud, 297*

The man or woman who lives worthily is now in a state of salvation.—*DBY, 391*

And if we accept salvation on the terms it is offered us, we have got to be honest in every thought, in our reflections, in our meditations, in our private circles, in our deals, in our declarations, and in every act of our lives, fearless and regardless of every principle of error, of every principle of falsehood that may be presented.—*JD, 5:124*

Is every man or woman capable of receiving the highest glory of God? No.—*DBY, 391*

If Brother Brigham shall take a wrong track, and be shut out of the Kingdom of heaven, no person will be to blame, but Brother Brigham. I am the only being in heaven, earth, or hell that can be blamed . . . Salvation is an individual operation.—*JD, 1:312*

You will be no more perfect in your sphere, when you are exalted to thrones, principalities, and powers, than you are required to be and are capable of being in your sphere today.—*JD, 6:99*

The economy of heaven is to gather in all, and save everybody who can be saved.—*DBY, 387*

People should understand that there is no man born upon the face of the earth but what can be saved in the Kingdom of God, if he is disposed to be.—*DBY, 387*

All heaven is anxious that the people be saved. The heavens weep over the people, because of their hard- heartedness, unbelief, and slowness to believe and act.—*DBY, 389*

All intelligent beings who are crowned with crowns of glory, immortality, and eternal lives must pass through every ordeal appointed for intelligent beings to pass through, to gain their glory and exaltation. Every calamity that can come upon mortal beings will be suffered to come upon the few, to prepare them to enjoy the presence of the Lord . . . Every trial and experience you have passed through is necessary for your salvation.—*JD, 8:150*

In the Millennium, when the Kingdom of God is established on the earth in power, glory and perfection, and the reign of wickedness that has so long prevailed is subdued, the Saints of God will have the privilege of building their temples, and of entering into them, becoming, as it were, pillars in the temples of God, and they will officiate for their dead. Then we will see our friends come up, and perhaps some that we have been acquainted with here. If we ask who will stand at the head of the resurrection in this last dispensation, the answer is—Joseph Smith, Junior, the Prophet of God. He is the man who will be resurrected and receive the keys of the resurrection, and he will seal this authority upon others, and they will hunt up their friends and resurrect them when they shall have been officiated for, and bring them up. And we will have revelations to know our forefathers clear back to Father Adam and Mother Eve, and we will enter into the temples of God and officiate for them. Then man will be sealed to men until the chain is made perfect back to Adam, so that there will be a perfect chain of Priesthood from Adam to the winding-up scene.—*DBY, 116*

SATAN

The devil does not care how much religion there is on the earth; he is a great preacher, and to all appearances a great gentleman, and it is necessary that he should be, and that all his co-workers should be as like their great leader and master as possible. They have forsaken the fountain of living waters, and hewed them out cisterns, broken cisterns, that can hold no water.—*JD, 11:251*

Satan works upon the opposite principle; he seeks to destroy, would annihilate if he could, but only decomposes, disorganizes. Permit me to inquire what was his curse? It was, that he should not increase any more, but come to an end.—*JD, 1:116*

If we live so as to enjoy the spirit of the faith that we embraced, there is no danger of our being deceived.—*DBY, 71*

We could not do without him. If there had been no devil to tempt Eve, she never would have got her eyes opened. We need a devil to stir up the wicked on the earth to purify the Saints. Therefore let the devils howl, let them rage . . . let them go on in their work, and do you not desire to kill them, until they ought to be killed.—*JD, 1:170*

The power of the Devil is limited; the power of God in unlimited.—*JD, 3:267*

Show me one principle that has originated by the power of the Devil. You cannot do it. I call evil inverted good, or a correct principle made an evil use of.—*DBY, 69*

The Devil's forces are particularly marshalled against us.—*DBY, 69*

You need have no fear but the fear to offend God.—*JD, 4:369*

Who owns this earth? Does the Devil? No, he does not, he pretended to own it when the Savior was here, and promised it all to him if he would fall down and worship him; but he did not own a foot of land, he only had possession of it. He was an intruder, and is still; this earth belongs to him that framed and organized it, and it is expressly for his glory and the possession of those who love and serve him and keep his commandments.—DBY, 68

There are but two parties on the earth, one for God and the other for the world or the evil one. No matter how many names the Christian or heathen world bear, or how many sects and creeds may exist, there are but two parties, one for heaven and God, and the other will go to some other kingdom than the celestial kingdom of God.—*DBY, 70*

SCRIPTURES

*D*o you read the scriptures, my brethren and sisters, as though you were writing them a thousand, two thousand, or five thousand years ago? Do you read them as though you stood in the place of the men who wrote them? If you do not feel thus, it is your privilege to do so, that you may be as familiar with the spirit and meaning of the written word of God as you are with your daily walk and conversation, or as you are with your workmen or with your households.—*JD, 7:333*

We as Latter-day Saints have confessed before Heaven, before the heavenly hosts, and before the inhabitants of the earth, that we really believe the Scriptures as they are given to us, according to the best understanding and knowledge that we have of the translation, and the spirit and meaning of the Old and New Testaments.—*JD, 12:227*

The book of Doctrine and Covenants is given for the Latter-day Saints expressly for their everyday walk and actions.—*DBY, 128*

The people on every hand are inquiring, "What does this scripture mean, and how shall we understand this or that passage?" Now I wish, my brethren and sisters, for us to understand things precisely as they are, and not as the flitting, changing imagination of the human mind may frame them. The Bible is just as plain and easy of comprehension as the revelation which I have just read to you, if you understand the Spirit of God—the Spirit of Revelation, and know how the Gospel of salvation is adapted to the capacity of weak man.—*JD, 3:336*

SERVICE

I wish you to understand, however, that a man giving his means to build up the Kingdom of God is no proof to me that he is true in heart. I have long since learned, that a person may give a gift with an impure design.—*JD, 8:12-13*

Man may think, and some of them do, that we have a right to work for ourselves; but I say we have no time to do that in the narrow, selfish sense generally entertained when speaking about working for self, we have no time allotted to us here on the earth to work for ourselves in that sense; and yet when laboring in the most disinterested and fervent manner for the cause and Kingdom of God, it is all for ourselves. Though our time be entirely occupied in laboring for the advancement of the Kingdom of God on the earth we are in reality laboring most effectually for self, for all our interest and welfare, both in time and eternity, are circumscribed and bound up in that Kingdom.—*JD, 14:101*

Give your heart to God and your life to his service and this testimony will continually increase with you and will never grow dim, and your strength will increase with your increasing years until you will have passed away, and your faith in the lord and His work will be undivided.—*Jessee, 219*

SIN

*D*arkness and sin were permitted to come on this earth. Man partook of the forbidden fruit in accordance with a plan devised from eternity, that mankind might be brought in contact with the principles and powers of darkness, that they might know the bitter and the sweet, the good and the evil, and be able to discern between light and darkness, to enable them to receive light continually.— *JD, 7:158*

Aside from the revelations of our day, there is not knowledge enough to tell you why God suffered sin to come into the world. You have been told the reason why—that all intelligence must prove facts by their opposite.—*DBY, 76*

The law of God is pointed against sin and iniquity, and where they appear it is unbending in its nature and must, sooner or later, hold sovereign rule against them, or righteousness could never prevail.—*DBY, 77*

Paul asks, "Shall we sin that righteousness may abound?" No, there is plenty of sin without your sinning. We can have all the experience we need, without sinning ourselves, therefore we will not sin that good may come, we will not transgress the law of God that we may know the opposite. There is no necessity for such a course, for the world is full of transgression, and this people need not mingle up with it.—*DBY, 77*

SMITH, JOSEPH

(See Joseph Smith)

SELF-RELIANCE

(See Industry)

SPIRIT

*S*ome spirits are more noble than others; some are capable of receiving more than others. There is the same variety in the spirit world that you behold here, yet they are of the same parentage, of one Father, one God, to say nothing of who He is. They are all of one parentage, though there is a difference in the capacities and nobility, and each one will be called to fill the station for which he is organized; and which he can fill.—*JD, 268-69*

Inasmuch as our spirits are inseparably connected with the flesh, and, inasmuch as the whole tabernacle is filled with the spirit which God gave, if the body is afflicted, the spirit also suffers, for there is a warfare between the flesh and the spirit, and if the flesh overcomes, the spirit is brought into bondage, and if the spirit overcomes, the body is made free, and then we are free indeed, for we are made free by the Son of God.—*JD, 3:247*

Keep your spirits under the sole control of good spirits, and they will make your tabernacles honorable in the presence of God, angels, and men. If you will always keep your spirits in right subjection, you will be watching all the time, and never suffer yourselves to commit an act that you will be sorry for, and you can see that in all your life you are clear.—*JD, 5:328*

When the body is prepared, at the proper time, the spirit enters the tabernacle, and all the world of mankind in their reflections and researches must come to this conclusion, for the fact is they can come to no other— that when the mother feels life there is an evidence that the spirit from heaven has entered the tabernacle.—*JD, 18:258*

Spirits were begotten, born and educated in the celestial world, and were brought forth by celestial bodies. . . . The spirits before inhabiting bodies are as pure and holy as the angels or the gods, they know no evil. This, their first estate, is the commencement of their experience.—*JD, 18:258*

There is no spirit but what was pure and holy when it came here from the celestial world . . . none that were begotten by angels, or by any inferior being. They were not produced by any being less than our Father in heaven. He is the Father of our spirits; and if we could know, understand, and do His will, every soul would be prepared to return back into His presence. And when they get there, they would see that they had formerly lived there for ages, that they had previously been acquainted with every nook and corner, with the palaces, walks, and gardens; and they would embrace their

Father, and He would embrace them and say, "My son, my daughter, I have you again," and the child would say, "O my Father, my Father, I am here again."—*JD, 4:268*

SPIRIT OF GOD (CHRIST, TRUTH)

*T*he Gospel of Jesus Christ . . . teaches that it is the privilege of every Saint so to live and walk before their God, as to enjoy the light of the spirit of truth from day to day, from week to week, and from year to year through their whole lives.—*DBY, 14*

Their testimony was like fire in my bones; I understood the spirit of their preaching; I received that spirit; it was light, intelligence, power, and truth.—*McCloud, 31*

The Spirit of the Lord at this time rested upon the people in a powerful manner . . . insomuch that the Saints' hearts were filled with joy unspeakable; every power of their mind and nerve of their bodies was awakened.—*McCloud, 162*

What is it that enables our Elders to go forth and preach the Gospel? The Spirit of the Lord. This is their experience and testimony. What do they testify when they go forth? That the Gospel, as set forth in the Old and New Testaments, is true; that the plan of salvation, revealed by God through his prophets in ancient times, and in modern times through Joseph Smith, is true; and as they are enlightened and aided by the Spirit of the Lord, error must fall before them . . . How easy it is to sustain truth! How easy it is to sustain the doctrines of the Savior.—*McCloud, 80*

Brother Maeser, whatever you teach, even the multiplication tables, do it with the spirit of the Lord.—*McCloud, 271*

SPIRITUAL GIFTS

*T*he gift of taste is the gift of God, we can use that to feed and pamper the lusts of the flesh, or we can use it to the glory of God.—*JD, 3:364*

The gift of seeing with the natural eyes is just as much a gift as the gift of tongues. The Lord gave that gift and we can do as we please with regard to seeing; we can use the sight of the eye to the glory of God, or to our own destruction.—*JD, 3:364*

The Almighty has commenced his work of sending forth his angels from the heavens, and revealing his will. He gave us Joseph, and others, and bestowed the Holy Priesthood upon his servants. We are sharers in the gifts and graces that God has bestowed upon his people.—*McCloud, 234*

By a close application of the gifts bestowed upon us, we can secure to ourselves the resurrection of these bodies that we now possess, that our spirits inhabit, and when they are resurrected they will be made pure and holy; then they will endure to all eternity.—*JD, 3:364*

SPIRIT WORLD

When you lay down this tabernacle, where are you going? Into the spiritual world. Are you going into Abraham's bosom? No, not anywhere nigh there but into the spirit world. Where is the spirit world? It is right here. Do the good and evil spirits go together? Yes, they do. Do they both inhabit one kingdom? Yes, they do. Do they go to the sun? No. Do they go beyond the boundaries of the organized earth? No, they do not. They are brought forth upon this earth, for the express purpose of inhabiting it to all eternity. Where else are you going? Nowhere else, only as you may be permitted.—*JD, 3:369*

The spirits that dwell in these tabernacles on this earth, when they leave them go directly into the world of spirits. What! A congregated mass of inhabitants there in spirit, mingling with each other, as they do here? Yes, brethren, they are there together, and if they associate together, and collect together, in clans and in societies as they do here, it is their privilege. No doubt they yet, more or less, see, hear, converse and have to do with each other, both good and bad. If the Elders of Israel in these latter times go and preach to the spirits in prison, they associate with them, precisely as our Elders associate with the wicked in the flesh, when they go to preach to them.—*JD, 2:137*

No spirit of Saint or sinner, of Prophet or him that kills the Prophet, is prepared for their final state; all pass through the veil from this state and go into the world of spirits; and there they dwell waiting for their final destiny.—*JD, 6:294*

When we pass into the spirit world we shall possess a measure of his power. Here, we are continually troubled with ills and ailments of various kinds. In the spirit world we are free from all this and enjoy life, glory, and intelligence; and we have the Father to speak to us, Jesus to speak to us, and angels to speak to us, and we shall enjoy the society of the just and the pure who are in the spirit world until the resurrection.—*DBY, 381*

We have more friends behind the veil than on this side, and they will hail us more joyfully than you were ever welcomed by your parents and friends in this world; and you will rejoice more when you meet them than you ever rejoiced to see a friend in this life; and then we shall go on from step to step, from rejoicing to rejoicing, and from one intelligence and power to another, our happiness becoming more and more exquisite and sensible as we proceed in the words and powers of life.—*JD, 6: 349*

STUDY

We try to live so as to gain more information, more light, more command over ourselves . . . until we can comprehend the great principles of existence and eternal progression. JD, 9:167

It is your duty to study to know everything upon the face of the earth, in addition to reading those books [the scriptures]. We should not only study good, and its effects upon our race, but also evil, and its consequences.—*JD, 2:93,94*

I want to have schools to entertain the minds of the people and to draw them out to learn the arts and sciences. Send the old children and the young ones also; there is nothing I would like better than to learn chemistry, botany, geology, and mineralogy, so that I could tell what I walk on, the properties of the air I breathe, what I drink, etc.—*McCloud, 270*

Every true principle, every true science, every art, and the knowledge that men possess, or that they ever did or ever will possess, is from God. We should take pains and pride to . . . rear our children so that the learning and education of the world may be theirs.—*JD, 12:326*

TEACHING

*I*f parents will continually set before their children examples worthy of their imitation and the approval of our Father in Heaven, they will turn the current, and the tide of feelings of their children, and they, eventually, will desire righteousness more than evil.—*JD, 14:195*

Is it not a blessing to have schools in our community, where our teachers can teach our children correct principles, and impart to them education that will be useful?—*JD, 8:92*

If we teach righteousness, let us also practice righteousness in every sense of the word; if we teach morality, let us be moral; let us see to it that we preserve ourselves within the bounds of all the good which we teach to others. I am sure this course will be good to live by and die by, and when we get through the journey of life, here, what consolation it will be to us to know that we have done as we have wished others to do by us in all respects.—*JD, 11:130*

Teach your children from their youth, never to set their hearts immoderately upon an object of this world.—*DBY, 207*

TELESTIAL, TERRESTRIAL KINGDOMS

*T*his is the plan of salvation. Jesus will never cease his work until all are brought up to the enjoyment of a kingdom in the mansions of his Father, where there are many kingdoms and many glories, to suit the works and faithfulness of all men that have lived on the earth. Some will obey the celestial law and receive of its glory, some will abide the terrestrial and some the telestial, and others will receive no glory.—*JD, 13:76*

We are placed on this earth to prove whether we are worthy to go into the celestial world, the terrestrial, or the telestial or to hell, or to any other kingdom, or place, and we have enough of life given to us to do this.—*JD, 4:269*

TEMPLES

*S*uppose we are ready to go into the temples of God to officiate for our fathers and grandfathers—for our ancestors back for hundreds of years, who are all looking to see what their children are doing upon the earth. The Lord says, I have sent the keys of Elijah the Prophet—I have imparted that doctrine to turn the hearts of the fathers. Now, all you children, are you looking to the salvation of your fathers? Are you seeking diligently to redeem those that have died without the Gospel, inasmuch as they sought the Lord Almighty to obtain promises for you? For our fathers did obtain promises that their seed should not be forgotten. O ye children of the fathers, look at these things. You are to enter into the temples of the Lord and officiate for your forefathers.—*DBY, 408*

We are trying to save the living and the dead. The living can have their choice, the dead have not. Millions of them died without the Gospel, without the Priesthood, and without the opportunities that we enjoy. We shall go forth in the name of Israel's God and attend to the ordinances for them. And through the Millennium, the thousand years that the people will love and serve God, we will build temples and officiate therein for those who have slept for hundreds and thousands of years—those who would have received the truth if they had had the opportunity; and we will bring them up, and form the chain entire, back to Adam.—JD, 14:97

We build temples because there is not a house on the face of the whole earth that has been reared to God's name which will in anywise compare with his character, and that he can consistently call his house. There are places on the earth where the Lord can come and dwell, if he pleases. They may be found on the tops of high mountains, or in some cavern or places where sinful man has never marked the soil with his polluted feet.—JD, 394

If we are faithful enough to go back and build that great temple which Joseph has written about, and should the Lord acknowledge the labor of his servants, then watch, for you will see somebody whom you have seen before, and many of you will see him whom you have not seen before, but you will know him as soon as you see him.—*JD, 3:372*

TEMPTATION

*I*f I am tempted to speak an evil word, I will keep my lips locked together…I will keep bad feelings under and actually smother them to death, then they are gone. But as sure as I let them out they will live and afflict me. If I smother them in myself, if I actually choke them to death, destroy the life, the power, the vigor thereof, they will pass off and leave me clear of fault, and pure, so far as that is concerned; and no man or woman on earth knows that I have ever been tempted to indulge in wicked feelings. Keep them to yourselves.—*DBY, 80*

When the Devil cannot overcome an individual through temptation to commit wickedness, when he sees that a person is determined to walk in the line and travel straight forward into the celestial kingdom, he will adopt a course of flattery, will strive to exercise a pleasing influence and move along smoothly with him, and when he sees an opportunity he will try to turn him out of the way, if it is only to the extent of a hair's breadth.—*JD, 3:318*

As you advance in life you will find every position and occupation surrounded by its peculiar temptations, the great strength and bulwark against all of which is prayer to our Heavenly Father. Cultivate this spirit and you will find that it shall be a wall of fire around you and your glory in the midst of you. In its practice you will find a safeguard against the wiles of the adversary, and every good resolution will be fortified by it, and every seductive influence will lose its power to annoy you.—*Jessee, 270*

"Where do you get your testimony?" "We get it from heaven."—*JD, 12:208*

You and I must have the testimony of Jesus within us, or it is of but little use for us to pretend to be servants of God. We must have that living witness within us.—*JD, 4:368*

If I attain to the knowledge of all true principles that have ever existed, and do not govern myself by them, they will damn me deeper in hell that if I had never known anything about them.—*DBY, 429*

How are we to know the voice of the Good Shepherd from the voice of a stranger? . . .when an individual, filled with the Spirit of God, declares the truth of heaven, the sheep hear that, the Spirit of the Lord pierces their inmost souls and sinks deep into their hearts; by the testimony of the Holy Ghost light springs up within them, and they see and understand for themselves. This is the way the Gospel should be preached by every Elder in Israel, and by the power every hearer should hear;

and if we would know the voice of the Good Shepherd, we must live so that the Spirit of the Lord can find its way to our hearts.—*DBY, 431*

It is a special privilege and blessing of the holy Gospel to every true believer, to know the truth for himself.—*DBY, 429*

Much of the most important information is alone derived through the power and testimony of the Holy Ghost in the speaker, revealing itself to the understanding and spirit of the hearer. This is the only way you can convey a knowledge of the invisible things of God.—*JD, 8:41*

TIME

I told them that we brought nothing but knowledge to direct them in the labors and to teach them how to employ their time.

This is the greatest wealth we possess—to know how to direct our labors rightly, spending every hour advantageously for the benefit of our wives and children and neighbors.—*JD, 12:172*

Here is time, where is eternity? It is here, just as much as anywhere in all the expanse of space; a measured space of time is only a part of eternity.—DBY, 47

Do you understand that what the Lord performs in the Latter days will be done quicker than in the former days? He suffered Noah to occupy one hundred and twenty years in building the ark. Were he to command us to build an ark, he would not allow so long a time for completing it.—JD, 8:134

When was there a beginning? There never was one; if there was, there will be an end; but there never was a beginning, and hence there will never be an end; that looks like eternity. When we talk about the beginning of eternity, it is rather simple conversation, and goes far beyond the capacity of man.—*DBY, 47*

Mankind are organized of element, designed to endure to all eternity; it never had a beginning and never can have an end. There never was a time when this matter of which you and I are composed, was not in existence, and there never can be a time when it will pass out of existence, it cannot be annihilated.—*DBY, 290*

What have we? Our time. Spend it as you will. Time is given to you; and when this is spent to the best possible advantage, for promoting truth upon the earth, it is placed to our account, and blessed are you; but when we spend our time in idleness and folly it will be placed against us.—*JD, 19:75*

TITHING

We do not ask anybody to pay tithing, unless they are disposed to do so; but if you pretend to pay tithing, pay it like honest men.—*DBY, 177*

I like the term, because it is scriptural, and I would rather use it than any other. The Lord instituted tithing; it was practiced in the days of Abraham, and Enoch and Adam and his children did not forget their tithes and offerings . . . I want to say this much to those who profess to be Latter-day Saints—if we neglect our tithes and offerings we will receive the chastening hand of the Lord. We may just as well count on this first as last. If we neglect to pay our tithes and offerings we will neglect other things and this will grow upon us until the spirit of the Gospel is entirely gone from us, and we are in the dark, and know not whither we are going.—JD, *15:163*

One thing is required at the hands of this people, and to understand which there is no necessity for receiving a commandment every year, viz: to pay their tithing. I do not suppose for a moment, that there is a person in this Church, who is unacquainted with the duty of paying tithing, neither is it necessary to have revelation every year upon the subject. There is the Law—pay one-tenth.—*JD, 1:278*

If we live our religion, we will be willing to pay tithing.—*JD, 10:283*

It is very true that the poor pay their tithing better than the rich do. If the rich would pay their tithing we should have plenty. The poor are faithful and prompt in paying their tithing, but the rich can hardly afford to pay theirs—they have too much . . . they wait and continue waiting, until, finally, the character comes along who is called Death, and he slips up to them and takes away their breath, then they are gone and cannot pay their tithing, they are too late, and so it goes.—*JD, 15:163-64*

What object have I in saying to the latter-day Saints, do this, that or the other? It is for my own benefit, it is for your benefit; it is for my own wealth and happiness, and for your wealth and happiness that we pay tithing and render obedience to any requirement of Heaven.—*JD, 16:114*

TRIALS (& TRIBULATIONS)

*W*e must have our day of trial—an opportunity to become acquainted with the bitter and the sweet. We are so organized as to be able to choose or to refuse . . . This is a day of trial; our faith and patience can now be tried: now is the time for your fortitude and integrity to be tried. Let the trials come: for if we should be so unspeakably happy as to obtain a crown of eternal life, we shall be like gold tried seven times in the fire. Let the fiery furnace burn, and the afflictions come, and the temptations be presented;—if we wish to be crowned with crowns of glory and exalted to dwell with our elder brother Jesus Christ, we must choose the good and refuse the evil.—*JD, 7:203*

The Lord has led this people through scenes of sorrow and affliction . . . I can say that I do not consider that I have ever suffered anything for this kingdom—nothing in the least.—*JD, 8:67*

Wake up, wake up, dear brethren . . . to the present glorious emergency in which the God of heaven has placed you to prove your faith.— *McCloud, 138*

The people of the Most High God must be tried. It is written that they will be tried in all things, even as Abraham was tried. If we are called to go upon mount Moriah to sacrifice a few of our Isaacs, it is no matter; we must just as well do that as anything else. I think there is a prospect for the Saints to have all the trials they wish for, or can desire.—*DBY, 345*

If we have correct doctrines, and will fashion our lives to them, we may sanctify ourselves without being chastened.—*DBY, 345*

Do I acknowledge the hand of the Lord in persecution? Yes, I do. It is one of the greatest blessings that could be conferred upon the people of the Lord.—*JD, 2:7*

All hell is moved against this people, because we are of one heart and of one mind.—*JD, 5:228*

As to trials, why bless your hearts, the man or woman who enjoys the spirit of our religion has no trials!—*DBY, 348*

This is a world in which we are to prove ourselves. The lifetime of man is a day of trial, wherein we may prove to God—in our darkness, in our weakness, and where the enemy reigns—that we are our Father's friends.—*McCloud, 299*

TRUTH

*T*ruth, wisdom, power, glory, light, and intelligence exist upon their own qualities . . . Truth is congenial with itself, and light cleaves to light . . . Truth cleaves to truth because it is truth; and it is to be adored, because it is an attribute of God, for its excellence, for itself.—*JD, 1:117*

Truth is an attribute of the nature of God. By it he is sanctified and glorified. Jesus Christ proceeded from his Father. He is called His "only begotten Son," and inherited germs of His Father's perfections and the attributes of his Father's nature, so that he sinned not. So with us; if the attributes of our nature become refined and regenerated by the truth, our offspring must inherit those perfections, more or less.—*JD, 11:209*

The Gospel is a fountain of truth, and truth is what we are after. We have embraced the truth— namely, the Gospel of the Son of God.—*DBY, 9*

The faithful love the truth, though it may be told in the most simple manner; it is sweeter to them than honey or the honey comb; they are no more afraid of it than they would be afraid of eating a piece of good honey . . . Truth is the sanctifier of those who love it and are guided by it.—*JD, 11: 209*

Do you think that people will obey the truth because it is true, unless they love it? No, they will not. Truth is obeyed when it is loved. Strict obedience to the truth will alone enable people to dwell in the presence of the Almighty.—*JD, 7:55*

Truth will abide when error passes away. Life will remain when they who have rejected the words of eternal life are swallowed up in death. I like the truth because it is true, because it is lovely and delightful, because it is so glorious in its nature, and so worthy the admiration, faith and consideration of all intelligent beings in heaven or on the earth.—*DBY, 9*

UNITY

*T*he faith of the Gospel of Jesus Christ is calculated to unite the people in one, and to bring them back to the unity and faith of those who obeyed the Gospel anciently, and finally to bring them back to glory.—*JD, 5:228*

If we are united, we are independent of the powers of hell and of the world.—*JD, 5:257*

Who can resist the power possessed by the Latter-day Saints in their union? And the stronger our union, the more mighty are the bands of our strength.—*DBY, 283*

Would you like to live at ease and get rich? Would you like to keep your homes in this city? I know you would. You can do so by being one in all things.—*DBY, 283*

I wish the people to understand that they have no interest apart from the Lord our God. The moment you have a divided interest, that moment you sever yourselves from eternal principles.—*McCloud, 299*

WEALTH

*D*o not be anxious to have this people become rich, and possess the affection of the world. I have been fearful lest we come to fellowship the world.—*JD, 10:298*

There is any amount of property, and gold and silver in the earth and on the earth, and the Lord gives to this one and that one—the wicked as well as the righteous—to see what they will do with it, but it all belongs to him. He has handed over a goodly portion to this people, and, through our faith, patience and industry, we have made us good, comfortable homes here, and there are many who are tolerably well off, and if they were in many parts of the world they would be called wealthy. But it is not ours, and all we have to do is to try and find out what the Lord wants us to do with what we have in our possession, and then go and do it.—*JD, 16:10*

Look out, ye men of Israel, and be careful that you love not the world or the things of the world in their present state, and in your loftiness and pride, forget the Lord your God. We ought to care no more for the silver and the gold, and the property that is so much sought for by the wicked world, than for the soil or the gravel upon which we tread.—*JD, 11:18*

How the Devil will play with a man who so worships gain!—*JD, 10:174*

Few men know what to do with riches when they possess them.—*JD, 1:250*

Men and women who are trying to make themselves happy in the possession of wealth or power will miss it, for nothing short of the Gospel of the Son of God can make the inhabitants of the earth happy, and prepare them to enjoy heaven here and hereafter.—*JD, 11:329*

The question will not arise with the Lord, nor with the messengers of the Almighty, how much wealth a man has got, but how has he come by this wealth and what will he do with it?— JD, 11:294

It is a disgrace to every man and woman who has sense enough to live, not to take care of their own relatives, their own poor, and plan for them to do something they are able to do.—*JD, 8:145*

The Latter-day Saints who turn their attention to money-making soon become cold in their feelings toward the ordinances of the house of God. They neglect their prayers, become unwilling to pay any donations; the law of tithing gets too great a task for them; and they finally forsake their God, and the providences of heaven seem to be shut from them—all in consequence of this lust after the things of this world, which will certainly perish in handling, and in their use they will fade away and go from us.—*DBY, 315*

WICKED (WICKEDNESS)

*T*he wicked cannot do anything against the truth. Every move they make to crush the Kingdom of God will be attended with the signal blessings of the Almighty for its further extension and ultimate triumph. All their efforts will result in the overthrow of sin and iniquity, and the increase of righteousness and the Kingdom of God upon the earth.—*JD, 8:175*

Cease to mingle with the wicked. Many of our Elders seem to believe that Christ and Baal can yet be made friends . . . It cannot be done; it never was done, and never can be accomplished. One or the other must reign triumphantly on the earth, and I say that Jesus Christ shall reign, and I will help him; and Baal shall not reign here much longer—the Devil shall not have power much longer upon the land of Joseph.—*JD, 8:325-26*

Recollect, brethren and sisters, every one of you, that when evil is suggested to you, when it arises in your hearts, it is through the temporal organization. When you are tempted, buffeted, and step out of the way inadvertently; when you are overtaken by a fault, or commit an over act unthinkingly; when you are full of evil passion, and wish to yield to it, then stop and let the spirit, which God has put into your tabernacles, take the lead. If you do that, I will promise that you will overcome all evil, and obtain eternal lives. But many, very many, let the spirit yield to the body, and are overcome and destroyed.—*DBY, 70*

Can you mingle with the wicked and feel contented in their company? If you can you are on the road to destruction.—*JD, 12:220*

Who are the evildoers? Those who have had the light presented to them, and rejected it.—*JD, 8:357*

WISDOM

*L*et wisdom be sown in your hearts, and let it bring forth a bountiful harvest. It is more profitable to you than all the gold and silver and other riches of earth. Let wisdom spring up in your hearts, and cultivate it.—*JD, 8:140*

The person who applies his heart to wisdom, and seeks diligently for understanding, will grow to be mighty in Israel.—*JD, 3:363*

Now, I ask the wise, where did you get your wisdom? Was it taught you? Yes, I say it was taught you. By your professors in college? No, it was taught you by the influence of the spirit that is in man, and the inspiration of the Spirit of God giveth it understanding; and every creature can thus add intelligence to intelligence.—*JD, 13:172*

If you cannot provide for your natural lives, how can you expect to have wisdom to obtain eternal lives? God has given you your existence—your body and spirit, and has blest you with ability, and thereby laid the foundation of all knowledge, wisdom, and understanding, and all glory and eternal lives. If you have not attained ability to provide for your natural wants, and for a wife and a few children, what have you to do with heavenly things?"—*JD, 8:68*

After all our endeavors to obtain wisdom from the best books, etc., there still remains an open fountain for all: "If any man lack wisdom let him ask of God." Let every Latter-day Saint constantly practice himself in the performance of every good word and work, to acknowledge God to be God, to be strict in keeping his laws, and learning to love mercy, eschew evil and delight in constantly doing that which is pleasing to God. This is the only sure way to obtain influence with God and with all good men.—*JD, 9:370*

WOMEN

Now, sisters, I want you to vote also, because women are the characters that rule the ballot box.—*JD, 1:218*

Office and priesthood carry heavy responsibilities requiring constant labour and time. No woman could safely carry the triple burden of wifehood, motherhood, and at the same time of functioning in priestly orders. Yet her creative home labour ranks side by side, in earthly and heavenly importance, with her husband's priestly responsibilities. His in the market-place—hers at the hearthstone. He is the leader and she follows, not because she must, but because she wills to do so. She chooses to magnify her sphere as he chooses his.—*Gates/Widtsoe, 195-96*

Susa: A measure of public activity for all women, single or married, was encouraged, but only as it would help to broaden and increase their capacity as home-makers and mothers. This is the creative physical and spiritual labour which makes woman approach nearest to Godhood. Said he on one occasion to an ambitious daughter who had been appointed to go out and lecture with others throughout the country: "Daughter, use all your gifts to build up righteousness in the earth. Never use them to acquire name or fame. Never rob your home, nor your children. If you were to become the greatest woman on earth and your name should be known in every land and clime, but you should neglect your home and family, you would wake up in the morning of the resurrection and find you had failed in everything! However, after

Brethren and sisters, if we wish the blessings of heaven upon us, let us be faithful to our covenants and callings, faithful in paying tithing, in keeping the Word of Wisdom and in building temples.—*JD, 16:69*

Instead of doing two days' work in one day, wisdom would dictate to our sisters, and to every other person, that if they desire long life and good health, they must, after sufficient exertion, allow the body to rest before it is entirely exhausted. When exhausted, some argue that they need stimulants in the shape of tea, coffee, spirituous liquors, tobacco, or some of those narcotic substances which are often taken to goad on the lagging powers to greater exertions. But instead of these kinds of stimulants they should recruit by rest. Work less, wear less, eat less, and we shall be a great deal wiser, healthier, and wealthier people than by taking the course we now do.—*DBY, 188*

This Word of Wisdom which has been supposed to have become stale, and not in force, is like all the counsels of God, in force as much today as it ever was. There is life, everlasting life in it—the life which now is and the life which is to come.— *DBY, 184*

Tobacco, whether used in smoking or chewing, is an unmitigated evil to young men, injuring their health, impairing their mental powers and unfitting them for their daily duties and studies . . . Some young men seem to entertain the idea that to smoke, chew, or to use profane language makes them appear more manly. Never was there a greater fallacy. [Real] manhood is manifested in serving God and keeping his commandments. . . . If boys wish to be thought manly, let them copy the best men and their virtues, not inferior and vicious men and their follies and vices.—*Jessee, 308-309*

WORDS OF OTHERS ABOUT BRIGHAM YOUNG

*S*usa on her father's early life: He cultivated contact with intelligent men older than himself, yet retained lively relationships with youth. Always fond of children, he drew them naturally into the radius of his magnetic friendship. As a youth, he gathered little boys around him, telling them patriotic stories, inciting them to deeds of valour, and raising their ideals of life.—*McCloud, 17*

Dr. Ellis Shipp: How kind and fatherly Brigham Young was to me. My heart warms and my eyes moisten to the big heart, the generous consideration of that great man who lived to bless all the world as far as mortal power could reach. Directed by what seemed a divine instinct he could read and understand the human heart. His vision could encompass all of mortal need in the great and vital things, and even unto the smallest detail of everyday life.—*McCloud, 17-18*

Recollections of a Canandaigua citizen: There could scarcely be a more kind and affectionate husband and father than he [Brigham] was, and few men in his circumstances would have provided better for their families. Mrs. Young was sick, most of the time unable to do any kind of work, but she was a worthy woman, and an exemplary Christian; she was well deserving of his care and attention, and she had it while she lived in Canandaigua . . . We never thought him fanatical . . . he was looked upon by his neighbors generally to be a consistent Christian.—*McCloud, 22-23*

Richard Burton, upon meeting Brigham Young: The first impression on my mind by this short visit, and it was subsequently confirmed, was that the Prophet is no common man and that he has none of the weakness and vanity which characterize the common man.—*McCloud, 220*

Brigham's record of a statement by the Prophet Joseph Smith: In the evening a few of the brethren came in and conversed together upon the things of the Kingdom. He [Joseph] called upon me to pray; in my prayer I spoke in tongues. As soon as we arose from our knees the brethren flocked around him, and asked his opinion concerning the gift of tongues that was upon me. He told them that it was the pure Adamic language. Some said to him they expected he would condemn the gift brother Brigham had, but he said, "No, it is of God, and the time will come when Brother Brigham Young will preside over this Church." The latter part of this conversation was in my absence.—*McCloud, 41*

Dr. Hugh Nibley: I feel a mental midget to the side of Brigham Young . . . I am thinking of the two great men of our dispensation, the one the devoted disciple and boundless admirer of the other—Joseph Smith and Brigham Young. They are practically out of reach as exemplary figures.—*McCloud, 299*

Richard Burton: . . . fifty-nine years of age: he looks about forty-five . . . Scarcely a gray thread appears in his hair, which is parted on the side, light coloured, rather thick, and reaches below the ears with a half curl . . . The forehead is somewhat narrow, the eyebrows are thin, the eyes between grey and blue, with a calm, composed and somewhat reserved expression . . . His manner is at once affable and impressive, simple and courteous . . . He shows no signs of dogmatism, bigotry, or fanaticism . . . He impresses the stranger with a certain sense of power . . . He is neither morose nor methodistic, and where occasion requires he can use all the weapons of ridicule to direful effect, and 'speak a bit of his mind' in a style which no one forgets . . . His powers of observation are intuitively strong, and his friends declare him to be gifted with an excellent memory and a perfect judgment of character.—*McCloud, 243*

Recollections of Clarissa, Brigham's fifty-first child: He was good to look at, and I fail to recall an instance when he was not immaculate in person and dress. He had well-shaped hands and feet, a clear white skin, and blue eyes—the kind that radiate love and tenderness—and a mouth that was firm, commanding the respect of all with whom he came in contact. Few could resist the wonderful personality that made him so beloved of his people. He was of medium height, rather large, with beautiful light brown curly hair, a high brow that was broad and intelligent, a long straight nose, and a chin that denoted character and firmness.—*McCloud, 243*

John Taylor: President Young's memory is remarkable in regard to names and persons. I have traveled with him throughout the length and breadth of this Territory, and I do not know that I have ever seen him come in contact with a man whose name he did not remember and the circumstances connected with him. There is something remarkable in this.—*McCloud, 284*

Susa: As a young man my father chewed tobacco. In after years he told the story of that conquered appetite. "I carried a half plug of tobacco in my pocket for a long time," he said. "When the gnawing for it seemed unbearable I would take it out, look at it, and say, 'Are you, or is Brigham going to be master? Then it went back untouched into my pocket." He denounced the liquor traffic and all drunkenness. "If I had the influence the world gives me credit for," he once said, "I would not have a single drunkard, thief, or liar in this society. I do not profess to have that influence, but I can raise my voice against these evils."—*Gates/Widtsoe, 333*

Jedediah M. Grant, counselor to President Young: How is it that brother Brigham is able to comfort and soothe those who are depressed in spirit, and always make those with whom he associates so happy? I will tell you how he makes us feel so happy. He is happy himself, and the man who is happy himself can make others feel so, for the light of God is in him, and others feel the influence, and feel happy in his society.—*McCloud, 195*

Susa: This great leader was so just, so true, so genuine in his domestic relations that those who came into the household to assist, either within the confines of the house itself or without . . . felt that each "belonged" to him and his family. Each man, each woman became a very part of Brigham Young's life and were interwoven into the domestic fabric for ever. Two of his daughters married his business manager, another married the telegraph clerk in his office, another his teamster, while still another married a salesman in the shop.— *Gates/Widtsoe, 339*

Mrs. Kane: He wore a great surtout, reaching almost to his feet . . . and a pair of sealskin boots with the undyed fur outward. I was amused at his odd appearance; but as he turned to address me, he removed a hideous pair of green goggles, and his keen, blue-gray eyes met mine with their characteristic look of shrewd and cunning insight. I felt no further inclination to laugh. His photographs, accurate enough in other respects, altogether fail to give the expression of his eyes.—*McCLoud, 285*

B.F. Grant: My recollection of President Young was that he had two great outstanding personalities; one a very stern and positive way of saying and doing things, and at other times he had a kind and loving way that would be worthy of a loving mother for her child. However, he was possessed of that wonderful spirit of discernment that it seemed to me, at all times he was able to decide which of these attitudes to use in order that justice and right should prevail . . . I would to God I had the ability and words to express my great appreciation and love for this great Pioneer who led his people, under the inspiration and direction of Almighty God . . . God bless his memory and posterity to the last generation of time.—*McCloud, 290-91*

WORK

(See Labor)

WORDLINESS
OR THE WORLD

*H*ow gladly would we understand every principle pertaining to science and art, and become thoroughly acquainted with every intricate operation of nature, and with all the chemical changes that are constantly going on around us! How delightful this would be, and what a boundless field of truth and power is open for us to explore! We are only just approaching the shores of the vast ocean of information that pertains to this physical world, to say nothing of that which pertains to the heavens, to angels and celestial beings, to the place of their habitation, to the manner of their life, and their progress to still higher degrees of perfection.—*JD, 9:167*

We should be a people of profound learning pertaining to the things of the world. We should be familiar with the various languages, for we wish to send missionaries to the different nations and to the islands of the sea. We wish missionaries who may go to France to be able to speak the French language fluently, and those who may go to Germany, Italy, Spain, and so on to all nations, to be familiar with the languages of those nations.—*DBY, 254*

Men are greedy for the vain things of this world. In their hearts they are covetous. It is true that the things of this world are designed to make us comfortable, and they make some people as happy as they can be here; but riches can never make the Latter-day Saints happy. Riches of themselves cannot produce permanent happiness; only the Spirit that comes from above can do that.—*JD, 7:135*

WORSHIP

*C*oming to this Tabernacle to worship and do the will of God for one day in the week, and following our own inclinations and doing our own will at all other times, is a folly; it is useless, and a perfect burlesque on the service of God. We should do the will of God, and spend all our time for the accomplishment of his purposes, whether we are in this Tabernacle or elsewhere.—*JD, 12:34*

Worship on Every Day—Monday, Tuesday, Wednesday, Thursday, Friday and Saturday must be spent to the glory of God, as much as Sunday, or we shall come short of the object of our pursuit.—*JD, 13:261*

I would as soon see a man worshiping a little god made of brass or of wood as to see him worship his property.—*JD, 6:196*

When people assemble to worship they should leave their worldly cares where they belong, then their minds are in a proper condition to worship the Lord, to call upon him in the name of Jesus, and to get his Holy Spirit, that they might hear and understand things as they are in eternity, and know how to comprehend the providences of our God. This is the time for their minds to be open, to behold the invisible things of God, that he reveals by his Spirit.—*JD, 3:53*

YOUTH

I say to our young men, be faithful, for you do not know what is before you, and abstain from bad company and bad habits. Let me say to the boys sixteen years old and even younger, make up your minds to mark out the path of rectitude for yourselves, and when evil is presented, let it pass unnoticed by you, and preserve yourselves in truth, in righteousness, virtue and holiness before the Lord. You were born in the Kingdom of God; it is to be built up; the earth has to be renovated, and the people sanctified, after they are gathered from the nations, and it requires considerable skill and ability to do this; let our young men prepare themselves to aid and do their part in this great work. I want you to remember this teaching with regard to our youth.—*JD, 11:118*

There is need for the young daughters of Israel to get a living testimony of the truth. I wish our girls to obtain a knowledge of the gospel for themselves. I want you to vote to retrench in your dress, in your tables, in your speech, wherein you have been guilty of silly, extravagant speeches and light-mindedness of thought. Retrench in everything that is not good and beautiful. Not to make yourselves unhappy, but to live so that you may be truly happy in this life and in the life to come.—*McCloud, 268-69*

You have everything to encourage you, for heaven and good men are on your side, and you know the saying, "heaven and one good man is a large majority." You have just started out and your future is in a great measure depending upon your course now. Be diligent and prayerful. It is your privilege to know for yourself God lives and that He is doing a work in these last days and we are His honored ministers. Live for this knowledge and you will receive it. Remember your prayers and be fervent in spirit. Shun the very appearance of evil. . . trust in God.—*Jessee, 245*

ZION

*E*verything connected with building up Zion requires actual, severe labor. It is nonsense to talk about building up any kingdom except by labor; it requires the labor of every part of our organization, whether it be mental, physical, or spiritual, and that is the only way to build up a Kingdom of God.—*JD, 3:122*

If we wish to enjoy the Spirit of Zion, we must live for it. Our religion is not merely theory; it is a practical religion, to bring present enjoyment to every heart.—*JD, 8:33*

This American continent will be Zion; for it is so spoken of by the prophets. Jerusalem will be rebuilt and will be the place of gathering, and the tribe of Judah will gather there; but this continent of America is the land of Zion.—*JD, 5:4*

We have no business here other than to build up and establish the Zion of God. It must be done according to the will and law of God, after that pattern and order by which Enoch built up and perfected the former-day Zion, which was taken away to heaven, hence the saying went abroad that Zion had fled. . . . As Enoch prepared his people to be worthy of translation, so we, through our faithfulness, must prepare ourselves to meet Zion from above when it shall return to earth, and to abide the brightness and glory of its coming.—*JD, 18:356*

When we conclude to make a Zion we will make it, and this work commences in the heart of each person. When the father of a family wishes to make a Zion in his own house, he must take the lead in this good work, which it is impossible for him to do unless he himself possesses the spirit of Zion. Before he can produce the work of sanctification in his family, he must sanctify himself, and by this means God can help him to sanctify his family.—*JD, 9:283*

Zion will extend, eventually, all over this earth. There will be no nook or corner upon the earth but what will be in Zion. It will all be Zion.—*JD, 9:138*

I have Zion in view constantly . . . Our work is to bring forth Zion, and produce the Kingdom of God in its perfection and beauty upon the earth . . . When the wicked have power to blow out the sun, that it shines no more; when they have power to bring to a conclusion the operations of the elements, suspend the whole system of nature . . . then they may think to check "Mormonism" . . . and thwart the unalterable purposes of heaven . . . Jehovah is the "Mormonism" of this people, their Priesthood and their power.—*McCloud, 3*